101 Conditioning Games and Drills for Athletes

Jay Dawes, M.S.

Chris Mooney, M.S.

COACHES CHOICE™

ISBN: 978-1-58518-987-8
Library of Congress Control Number: 2006929424

Book layout: Bean Creek Studio
Diagrams: April Dawes
Cover design: Studio J Art & Design

Coaches Choice
P.O. Box 1828
Monterey, CA 93942
www.coacheschoice.com

Acknowledgments

The authors would like to thank the athletes and models from the University of Central Oklahoma, John Browning for his assistance in the copyediting of this manuscript, Jenn Mooney for her support and assistance in various capacities during the completion of this manuscript, and April Dawes for creating the diagrams featured in this work, and for providing her professional expertise and support throughout this process.

Contents

Introduction

Developing a solid fitness base is critical for anyone striving to achieve higher levels of performance. While most athletes realize that physical fitness can significantly improve athletic ability, many still dread participating in structured strength and conditioning routines. Unfortunately, many athletes perceive traditional training as a monotonous chore to be endured. This perception often leads to feelings of boredom, staleness, apathy, and, in many cases, a decrease in the effort exerted during training sessions. For this reason, coaches must continually seek new and innovative ways to motivate and challenge their athletes to strive for optimal athletic conditioning.

In recent years, the use of skill-based and competitive game play has gained a great deal of attention as a method of conditioning and developing various movement and sport-specific skills in team-sport athletes (Gabbet, 2002; Gamble, 2004; Jeffereys, 2004; Jeffereys, 2005a,b; Morgan-Handzel, 2005; Sherman, 1998). Some of the benefits associated with the use of these games include:

- Improvements in physical fitness, including cardiorespiratory endurance, muscular strength/endurance, flexibility, and body composition
- Improvements in the skill-related components of fitness, including agility, balance, coordination, power, speed, and reaction time
- Creation of a competitive environment in which athletes perform under pressure and fatigue common during an actual athletic contest
- Greater time efficiency by combining specific sport-related skills and conditioning routines
- Variety in the conditioning routine
- Improvements in motivation, enthusiasm, and intensity during conditioning sessions
- Facilitation of enjoyment

As previously stated, athletes often become bored with conditioning programs that focus on the use of conventional training methods based on sets, repetitions, specific work-to-rest ratios, and steady-state aerobic activities, in addition to separately training for each component of health/fitness. While it is not our intention to deemphasize the necessity and value of these traditional methods of training, the use of skill-based and competitive games, when appropriately combined with these protocols and modalities, can have a significant impact on the overall training program. These types of games disguise "work" as "play" and shift the primary emphasis of training sessions from attaining and maintaining certain training intensities to competition, teamwork, and enjoyment!

Game/Drill Selection

To gain a more comprehensive understanding of how the use of skill-based and competitive games can improve various aspects of physical fitness and various skills related to specific sports, a brief discussion of energy-system training and basic fundamental movement skills is necessary to ensure that the desired results of the training session are achieved.

Energy-System Training

The body relies on three energy systems to meet the physical demands placed upon it. These systems are the ATP-PCr (phosphocreatine), glycolytic (i.e., lactic acid and anaerobic), and oxidative (i.e., aerobic) systems.

The ATP-PCr energy system is arguably the simplest of these systems. This system is engaged during events that require approximately three to 15 seconds of high-intensity energy and are not oxygen-dependent, such as a 40-yard dash (Wilmore and Costill, 1999). For events requiring intense effort that must be sustained for greater than 15 seconds but less than two minutes (e.g., an 800-meter race), the glycolytic energy system is engaged. Finally the oxidative, or aerobic, energy system is engaged during events and competitions that are more steady-state in nature, such as distance running or cycling. While most sports and activities engage these systems in varying amounts during competition, the primary energy system engaged during a given activity or event results from the demands placed on the body to complete the skills or tasks required.

At the beginning of an activity, in theory the ATP-PCr is the first of these systems to be engaged. Once stored ATP is depleted, the body becomes more reliant on the other energy systems to sustain activity. The glycolytic or oxidative system begins to break down stored carbohydrates to produce ATP in an effort to sustain the work demands of the activity. This process is achieved through anaerobic glycolysis during intense activities lasting more than 15 seconds but less than two minutes, and through the oxidative system during longer-duration steady-state activities.

Anaerobic glycolysis does not utilize oxygen. Therefore, lactic acid is produced as a by-product. This process leads to high levels of metabolic waste products accumulating in the body, especially hydrogen (Wilmore and Costill, 1999). This increase in waste production, in conjunction with lactic-acid accumulation, causes the athlete to slow down after approximately one to two minutes of continuous activity (Wilmore and Costill, 1999).

The oxidative, or aerobic, system is the primary energy system engaged for activities requiring energy production that must be sustained for greater than two minutes. This system then demonstrates its ability to utilize oxygen to facilitate the breakdown of carbohydrates, fats, and proteins into energy.

Based on the concept of specificity, it is imperative that you have a fundamental understanding of these systems to effectively develop conditioning programs according to the needs of each individual sport. When selecting conditioning games, try to match the primary energy-system demands during competition. However, many athletic events fail to rely exclusively on one system. For example, soccer requires short bursts of explosive energy-focused activity, such as sprinting, followed by intervals of light- to moderate-intensity activities, such as jogging, to be in position for the next play. Soccer, therefore, requires a blending of all three energy systems to perform at an optimal level. Rather than working each system in isolation, selecting a game such as Everybody's It (#19) allows you to integrate all three systems in a manner similar to the actual competitive demands of the sport. This factor is important to consider when seeking to maximize the benefits of an athlete's training program, especially when the time available for conditioning is limited.

Fundamental Movement Skills

The basic fundamental movement skills include locomotor, nonlocomotor, manipulative, and movement/body awareness (Figure 1). According to Gambetta (1998), in the past these skills were primarily developed during free play and in physical-education classes. However, we are living in an era in which individuals are more sedentary and physical-education programs are being cut due to budgetary restraints. While the secret to athletic dominance is believed to stem from early sport specialization, physical-education programs are waning. As a result, many athletes may lack the proper "tools," or motor skills, that are necessary for competition or when learning sport-specific skills.

Locomotor	Nonlocomotor	Manipulative	Movement Awareness
Walking	Twisting	Throwing	Spatial
Running	Turning	Catching	Temporal
Skipping	Balancing	Kicking	Kinesthetic
Hopping	Jumping	Punting	
Sliding	Landing	Dribbling	
Chasing	Stretching	Striking	
Fleeing	Pushing	Volleying	
Dodging	Pulling		
Galloping			
Rolling			
Sources: Gambetta, 1998; Pangrazzi, 1998			

Figure 1. Fundamental movement skills

A large number of the games featured in this work are adapted from various physical-education games and resources that focus on the development of general fitness parameters and on the improvement of fundamental movement skills. Therefore, many games included in this work are not considered sport-specific, but are general conditioning games that emphasize "athletic movements" and the fundamental movement skills discussed earlier and listed in Table 1. To yield the greatest transfer of training effect, select activities that have similar biomechanical demands and movement patterns.

Adapting the Games/Drills

The games/drills contained in this work can be modified in various ways to increase or decrease the training intensity and/or skill requirements for each activity. The following suggestions will help you manipulate the various components of these games/drills.

Number of Athletes

Depending on the game/drill, decreasing or increasing the number of participating athletes can significantly increase the energy demands of the activity. For example, decreasing the number of athletes in relay-based and chasing/fleeing-type games/drills significantly increases the energy demands placed on each athlete, because he is required to perform more often. For example, a team of six athletes may only have time to run an obstacle course once, but a team of two or three athletes would have time to complete the course two or three times. Increasing the number of athletes can also increase the number of training stimuli available because an athlete must constantly be aware of what his teammates and opponents are doing to respond with accurate, precise, and appropriate actions.

Playing Area

The size of the playing area also impacts the intensity of the game/drill. If the playing area is too small or too large, the energy demands may be lessened, thus reducing the training effect of the activity. While the selected game/drill generally dictates the size of the playing area, the playing area can be increased or decreased to alter the intensity of the game/drill and allow you to emphasize specific energy systems. For example, a small playing area for Everybody's It tends to focus on the phosphate/glycolitic system, which may be more beneficial for sprint-based athletes. Conversely, increasing the size of the playing area puts more emphasis on the aerobic/glycolytic system, which may be more beneficial for athletes who are required to perform sustained activity for longer periods of time and perform sprints in short sporadic bursts throughout a competition, such as in basketball.

Incorporate Other Skills

Many of the games/drills can be adapted by simply incorporating new and different movement skills. However, before making any modifications, be certain that the games/drills are appropriate and safe (See "Basic Guidelines" in this Introduction for more information). Some examples of skills that can be incorporated into the framework of a game/drill are skips, hops (one or two feet), jumps, and running in various directions (i.e., forward, backward, sideways, or in place). You may also find it advantageous to add various sport-specific skills into games/drills to maximize practice time. For example, dribbling could be included for basketball or soccer athletes, while football athletes may participate in certain games/drills wearing full pads or helmets to acclimate themselves to moving in their equipment.

Work-to-Rest Ratios

Work-to-rest ratios can have a profound impact on the intensity of a game/drill. Too much or too little rest can negatively impact the conditioning effect. If too much rest is given, athletes are neither challenged nor forced to make a positive adaptation in response to the training stimulus. However, if the training stimulus is too great, the likelihood of injury increases and the appropriate metabolic training may not be achieved. The key to deciding the proper work-to-rest ratio for each game/drill is to determine how much time athletes need to recover in a normal competition. For instance, when training a football team, you may mix longer rest periods with shorter rest periods to resemble a "no-huddle" situation. This technique should condition the athletes in a way that is more specific to the physical demands they inevitably face on the playing field.

Player Selection

Various techniques can be implemented when selecting athletes. You may prefer to have athletes number-off to randomize the groups, or assign team captains and instruct athletes to "draft" or choose their teams. More importantly, make an effort to equalize the teams based on an athletes' size, strength, and abilities, which ensures that one team does not have an unfair competitive advantage that may reduce enthusiasm for the training by athletes on the opposing teams.

Basic Guidelines

The following list of basic guidelines will assist you in implementing skill-based and competitive games/drills into an athletic training program. This list is not intended to be comprehensive, but rather to provide general recommendations for maximizing safety and time utilization during training session, as well as for facilitating healthy competition among athletes.

- Try to keep teams evenly matched by pairing athletes according to strength, size, and physical abilities.

- Make every effort to ensure that all playing areas are free of sharp objects and clutter to maximize safety and reduce the risk of injury to athletes, coaches, and bystanders.

- Keep a fully stocked first aid kit readily available.

- Be sure that at least one coach with first aid and CPR training is present.

- Be sure that a certified lifeguard is on duty for all games/drills facilitated in a swimming pool.

- Keep everyone involved and do not allow athletes to stand around after they have been eliminated from a game/drill. Athletes left without specific tasks may engage in horseplay unless they remain occupied. This problem can be alleviated by requiring athletes to perform conditioning exercises while waiting for the next game to begin or perform a certain number of push-ups, jumping jacks, etc., before reentering the game. This technique also ensures that conditioning time is optimized.

- When giving directions to a group, make sure that everyone in that group is able to hear. You may also explain the rules of a drill/game to the team leader, thus giving him the responsibility of explaining the rules to the rest of his team.

- Be sensitive to when the athletes are becoming overly fatigued and adjust work-to-rest ratios accordingly. You can also combine strenuous games/drills with those that are less physically demanding.

- If a game/drill is not working, be flexible by being prepared to modify it. Frequently change the skill requirements, boundary lines, goals, and roles of certain athletes within the context of a game/drill to adjust the physical demands and the speed of play.

Incorporating Games/Drills into Practice and Training Sessions

It is important that you understand that these games/drills are not a panacea, but rather another tool that can be utilized to improve your athletes' abilities and fitness levels. Utilize the following recommendations for implementing these games/drills into a comprehensive training program:

- Use games/drills after the general or specific warm-up activity to prepare athletes for practice or other conditioning sessions.

- Use a game/drill as a stand-alone activity on days between training sessions or between competitions.

- Introduce games/drills during the active rest phases commonly used in periodization plans.

- Use games/drills that require fewer athletes between exercises or drills in a circuit.

Selecting a Specific Game/Drill to Meet a Specific Purpose

Games/drills can be used to develop a variety of fitness and motor-skill attributes—18 in all. Figure 2 details which attributes are developed by which game/drill. Coaches should select games that emphasize the specific skills and abilities they want the athletes to develop. For organizational purposes, the drills are presented in the book in alphabetical order by title.

Let the Games Begin

In conclusion, we hope that you find the games/drills described in this work to be beneficial in the development of a comprehensive conditioning program for your athletes. Good luck!

		Aerobic Conditioning	Anaerobic Conditioning	Agility	Balance	Cognitive Awareness	Coordination	Flexibility
#1	500	✓	✓	✓		✓		
#2	Bait and Switch	✓	✓	✓	✓		✓	
#3	Beat the Ball	✓	✓					
#4	Bodyguard	✓	✓	✓	✓		✓	
#5	Bronco Corral					✓		
#6	Catch a Thief	✓	✓	✓				
#7	Catch Us If You Can	✓	✓	✓	✓		✓	
#8	Chuck It	✓	✓	✓				
#9	Circle Dodgeball			✓			✓	
#10	Crab Soccer							
#11	Crossfire	✓	✓	✓	✓		✓	
#12	Dirty Dozen Relay	✓	✓					
#13	Dodge Basketball	✓	✓	✓			✓	
#14	Drag Race							
#15	Dragon's Treasure	✓	✓	✓				
#16	Eagle Walk						✓	✓
#17	Elimination			✓				
#18	End Zone Ball	✓	✓	✓				
#19	Everbody's It			✓				
#20	Fill 'er Up	✓	✓					
#21	Fill the Bucket	✓	✓					
#22	Fireman Relay	✓	✓		✓			
#23	Fistball	✓	✓	✓				
#24	Flamingo Pass	✓	✓	✓	✓		✓	
#25	Flip the Bear							
#26	Floor Touch Wrestle							
#27	Free for All	✓	✓	✓	✓		✓	
#28	Gauntlet	✓	✓	✓				
#29	Heads or Tails	✓	✓	✓				
#30	Hit 'n' Run	✓						
#31	Hole in One							
#32	Hop Tag	✓	✓					
#33	Hot Ball	✓	✓		✓		✓	
#34	I Got Your Number		✓	✓	✓		✓	
#35	In the Zone	✓	✓	✓	✓		✓	
#36	Invade and Conquer	✓	✓	✓				

Figure 2. Conditioning Games and Drills

Manipulative Skills	Muscular Endurance	Muscular Strength	Power	Reaction	Recovery	Speed	Stability	Strategy	Teamwork	Timing
			✓	✓						
				✓						
	✓	✓	✓						✓	
				✓					✓	
	✓	✓				✓				
✓				✓		✓				
✓				✓		✓				
				✓		✓				
✓	✓	✓					✓			
				✓						
	✓	✓								
				✓					✓	
	✓	✓	✓							
				✓						
	✓	✓								
				✓		✓				
						✓				
				✓		✓				
	✓	✓								
	✓	✓								
	✓	✓							✓	
✓				✓						
	✓	✓	✓	✓						
	✓	✓	✓				✓			
	✓	✓	✓				✓			
				✓						
				✓						
				✓						
				✓						
	✓	✓							✓	
	✓	✓	✓							
	✓	✓		✓						
				✓						
	✓	✓	✓							

		Aerobic Conditioning	Anaerobic Conditioning	Agility	Balance	Cognitive Awareness	Coordination	Flexibility
#37	Jigsaw Relay	✓	✓	✓		✓	✓	
#38	Junk Yard Wars	✓	✓	✓	✓		✓	
#39	Kickboard Relay	✓	✓		✓		✓	
#40	King Crab							
#41	King of the Mountain Tug-of-War				✓			
#42	Knee Slaps							
#43	Land Mine			✓				
#44	Launch Pad			✓	✓		✓	
#45	Leap Frog	✓	✓	✓				
#46	Lily Pad				✓			
#47	Load Up	✓	✓					
#48	Medicine Ball Four-Square			✓				
#49	Medicine Ball Hop Relay							
#50	Medicine Ball Run	✓	✓	✓				
#51	Medicine Ball Speed Throw							
#52	Medicine Ball Tennis	✓	✓	✓				
#53	Monkey See, Monkey Do	✓	✓	✓	✓		✓	
#54	Musketeers	✓	✓					
#55	Noodle Gladiators				✓			
#56	Out	✓	✓	✓	✓		✓	
#57	Pace Master	✓				✓		
#58	Pass Interference	✓	✓	✓	✓		✓	
#59	Pass Precision	✓		✓				
#60	Pay it Forward	✓	✓					
#61	Pepper						✓	
#62	Possession	✓	✓	✓				
#63	Power Ball	✓	✓	✓				
#64	Pull for Time Tug-of-War							
#65	Pull for the Cone Tug-of-War							
#66	Rectangle Madness		✓	✓	✓		✓	
#67	Relay Golf	✓						
#68	Rip City			✓				
#69	Rock Wrestle							
#70	Rooster Fight				✓			
#71	Scramble Tug-of-War							
#72	Sharks and Minnows	✓	✓	✓	✓		✓	

Figure 2. Conditioning Games and Drills (cont'd)

Manipulative Skills	Muscular Endurance	Muscular Strength	Power	Reaction	Recovery	Speed	Stability	Strategy	Teamwork	Timing
				✓					✓	
				✓						
	✓	✓								
	✓	✓	✓				✓			
	✓	✓	✓				✓			
				✓						
	✓	✓	✓							
	✓	✓		✓					✓	
	✓			✓						
								✓	✓	
	✓	✓								
✓			✓	✓						
			✓						✓	
	✓	✓								
	✓	✓	✓	✓		✓			✓	
	✓	✓	✓							
	✓	✓		✓	✓					
				✓					✓	✓
							✓			
	✓	✓		✓						
				✓					✓	
				✓					✓	
	✓	✓							✓	
				✓						
✓				✓						
✓						✓				
	✓	✓		✓		✓	✓			
	✓	✓		✓		✓	✓			
				✓					✓	
		✓	✓			✓			✓	
						✓				
	✓	✓	✓	✓			✓			
	✓	✓	✓				✓			
	✓	✓	✓	✓		✓	✓			
	✓	✓		✓						

		Aerobic Conditioning	Anaerobic Conditioning	Agility	Balance	Cognitive Awareness	Coordination	Flexibility
#73	Shoulder Wrestle				✓			
#74	Single-Leg Tug-of-War				✓			
#75	Sled Race	✓	✓					
#76	Smacks							
#77	Soccer Dodgeball			✓			✓	
#78	Sprint Tug-of-War							
#79	Squat War				✓			
#80	Stool Burner Race							
#81	Stubborn Mule				✓			
#82	Submerge and Retrieve	✓	✓					
#83	Sumo Wrestling	✓	✓	✓				
#84	Swimming Through Hoops	✓	✓	✓			✓	
#85	Swiss Ball War				✓			
#86	Swiss Ball Wrestle				✓			
#87	Team Keep Away	✓	✓	✓				
#88	Teammate Carry							
#89	T-Shirt Shuffle	✓						
#90	Tug Wrestle				✓			
#91	Twister		✓		✓		✓	
#92	Ultimate			✓				
#93	Ultimate Tag			✓				
#94	Ultimate Square Off		✓	✓	✓		✓	
#95	Upper-Body Blitz							
#96	Wall Ball			✓			✓	
#97	Water Polo	✓	✓	✓			✓	
#98	Water Weave	✓		✓		✓	✓	
#99	Whammy Ball	✓		✓			✓	
#100	Wheelbarrow Relay							
#101	X-Factor		✓	✓	✓		✓	

Figure 2. Conditioning Games and Drills (cont'd)

Manipulative Skills	Muscular Endurance	Muscular Strength	Power	Reaction	Recovery	Speed	Stability	Strategy	Teamwork	Timing
	✓	✓	✓				✓			
	✓	✓	✓				✓			
	✓	✓								
				✓						
				✓		✓				
	✓	✓	✓	✓		✓	✓			
	✓	✓	✓				✓			
	✓	✓								
	✓	✓	✓				✓			
	✓	✓								
	✓	✓	✓							
	✓	✓								
			✓				✓			
	✓	✓					✓			
				✓		✓				
	✓	✓								
	✓								✓	
	✓	✓	✓				✓			
	✓	✓		✓						
✓				✓		✓				
✓				✓		✓				
				✓					✓	
	✓	✓	✓							
✓						✓				
	✓	✓		✓					✓	
	✓	✓							✓	
				✓					✓	
	✓	✓					✓			
	✓	✓	✓	✓					✓	

101 Conditioning Games and Drills for Athletes

#1: 500

Skills Developed: Aerobic/anaerobic conditioning, agility, cognitive awareness, power, and reaction

Players: 8 or more

Playing Area: Large open area (preferably grass or resilient flooring)

Materials Needed: 1 football or other soft foam or rubber ball

Description: The objective of this game is to accumulate 500 points. One athlete is the thrower and the others are catchers. Depending on the size of the group and area being used, approximately 10 to 20 yards should separate the thrower from the catchers. At the whistle, the thrower throws the ball high into the air over the group while calling out a number (e.g., between 50 and 500). The athlete who catches the pass receives the allotted points. If the ball is dropped, then no points are awarded. The first athlete to accumulate 500 points becomes the new thrower and the previous thrower then joins the catchers. This game continues for a preselected duration of time or until all of the athletes have served as throwers.

Variations:

- Any ball thrown, whether caught or dropped, scores points. This variation functions as a great way to teach athletes to scramble and fight for possession of the ball.

- If the group is small, then you can simply increase the final point total (e.g., to 1000 points).

#2: Bait and Switch

Skills Developed: Aerobic/anaerobic conditioning, agility, balance, coordination, and reaction

Players: 12 or more

Playing Area: Large open area

Materials Needed: None

Description: Begin by instructing the athletes to form a large circle (5 to 10 feet from each other) in the center of the playing area (see figure). Then, select two athletes, one runner and one chaser, to step out of the circle and position themselves on opposite sides of the circle. At the whistle, the chaser attempts to catch the runner by running around and/or weaving in and out of the circle. The runner's job is to avoid being caught by either running and avoiding the chaser or running and standing in front of another athlete in the circle. If the runner stands in front of another athlete, the roles are then reversed. The runner then joins the circle, the athlete he stands in front of becomes the chaser, and the previous chaser becomes the runner. If the runner is caught, then he becomes the new chaser. The game continues until all of the athletes have had a chance to serve as the runner and/or chaser. A winner can be selected by keeping track of how long it takes each catcher to catch a runner (i.e., the quickest time wins).

Variations:

- Have the athletes form two circles and appoint two runners and two chasers.

- Positions the athletes on their stomachs in a push-up position. The runner and chaser are then allowed to run around and jump over the athletes.

Player formation for Bait and Switch

#3: Beat the Ball

Skills Developed: Aerobic/anaerobic conditioning, muscular strength/endurance, power, and teamwork

Players: 16 or more

Playing Area: Baseball/softball field or large open area (Figure A)

Materials Needed: 8 bases or cones, 1 medicine ball (5 to 15 pounds)

Description: Begin by spreading the bases evenly around the baseball/softball diamond. After the initial set-up, divide the athletes into two teams, designating one of the teams as "home" and the other as "away." Next, each athlete from the home team takes the field and stands next to a base. If a team consists of more than 8 athletes, assign two athletes per base (one as a backup). The away team then lines up near home plate. At the whistle, the home team passes the medicine ball from base to base as quickly as possible using a chest pass (Figure B). In the process, each athlete from the away team attempts to outrun the ball around the bases by running and tagging each of the eight bases with his foot or hand. If the athlete outruns the ball back to home plate, then a point is scored for his team. However, if the ball makes it back before the runner, he is called out. After three outs or seven points have been scored, the teams switch positions. This process is repeated for nine innings or until time is called (e.g., practice or class is over). The team with the most points wins.

Variations:

- To increase the physical demands of this game, have all athletes who are not running, throwing, or receiving the ball perform various conditioning exercises, such as bodyweight squats or jumping jacks.

- Use different throwing motions (e.g., underhand, overhand).

- Use a lighter or heavier ball.

- Increase or decrease the distance between the bases.

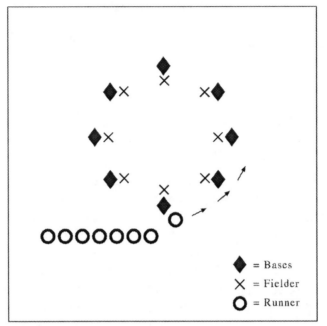

Figure A. Player formation for Beat the Ball

Figure B. Athlete performing a chest pass as the runner
attempts to beat the ball

#4: Bodyguard

Skills Developed: Aerobic/anaerobic conditioning, agility, balance, coordination, reaction, and teamwork

Players: 6 or more

Playing Area: Large open area with a 20-feet x 20-feet area in the center (see figure)

Materials Needed: 1 soft foam/rubber ball

Description: Begin by selecting two athletes, one to be the president and the other to be the bodyguard. These athletes are stationed inside the 20-feet x 20-feet area. All of the remaining athletes are then stationed on the outside of the area. At the whistle, the athletes stationed around the perimeter of the area throw the ball and attempt to "assassinate" the president. The bodyguard's job is to protect the president by deflecting or catching the balls. If the ball is caught, the thrower is declared out and must perform sit-ups, push-ups, or various other conditioning drills until the president has been replaced. If the president is hit, the bodyguard becomes the president and the thrower becomes the bodyguard. However, during this transition, play does not stop or slow down, so the athletes must remain on their toes. The game is played until all of the athletes have rotated out or have had an opportunity to be the president, or until time is up. A winner can be determined by keeping track of how many saves are made by each bodyguard. The athlete with the most saves is the winner.

Variations:

- Use two or more balls.

- Use a larger or smaller playing area.

- Appoint two presidents and one bodyguard (or vice versa).

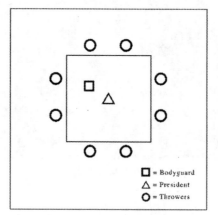

Player formation for Bodyguard

#5: Bronco Corral

Skills Developed: Muscular strength/endurance, speed, and balance

Players: 4 or more

Playing Area: Large open area

Materials Needed: 4 cones or markers

Description: This game is best played around a basketball court or football field with athletes of similar size and strength paired together. One athlete per pair is designated as the rider and the other as the bronco. Once the role for each athlete has been established, the rider should assume a piggyback position on the bronco (see figure). At the whistle, the bronco attempts to carry the rider around the playing area as quickly as possible. At each corner, the bronco must perform 10 to 20 squats with the rider still on his back, continue to the next corner as quickly as possible, and then repeat this process until he returns to the starting line. After each lap, the athletes switch positions before embarking on the next lap. If a bronco drops a rider during the race, both athletes must return to the last corner executed and reassume the piggyback position before proceeding to the next corner. The pair of athletes that is first to complete the number of laps predetermined by the coach wins.

Variations:

- Increase the number of laps performed by the athletes.

- Increase the number of squats to be performed at each corner.

A bronco performing a squat with the rider

#6: Catch a Thief

Skills Developed: Aerobic/anaerobic conditioning, agility, manipulative skills, speed, and reaction.

Players: 8 or more

Playing Area: Large open area (preferably a gymnasium)

Materials Needed: 6 medicine balls (same or various weights and sizes)

Description: Divide the athletes equally into two teams, with each team taking possession of half of the playing area. Position three medicine balls on the back line of each side (see figure). Once the game begins, the athletes attempt to capture the balls from the other team's side without being tagged. An athlete who successfully make it back to his side of the playing area with his opponent's ball and without being tagged may add the ball to his team's back line. Athletes tagged in the process of trying to capture their opponent's balls must go to jail and perform a predetermined series of exercises (e.g., push-ups, squats, lunges, sit-ups) until a teammate rescues them. Teammates may rescue prisoners by going into the jail and tagging them. Only one prisoner may be released from jail at a time. If the rescuer is tagged while in the process of freeing prisoners, then he too must go to jail and wait for rescue. The game is over when one team captures all of the opponent's balls or when all members of one team are captured.

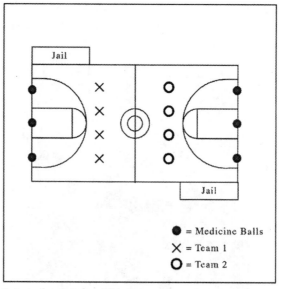

Set-up for Catch a Thief

Athlete performing tire flips during a relay

#7: Catch Us If You Can

Skills Developed: Aerobic/anaerobic conditioning, agility, balance, and coordination

Players: 4–8

Playing Area: Large open area

Materials Needed: 16 cones/markers (optional: agility ladders, hurdles, or medicine balls)

Description: Arrange the cones into stations, with each station containing four cones, at a distance of approximately 15 yards from each other in the shape of a square (Figure A). Once the field is set, divide the athletes into two teams. At stations 1 and 3, the athletes perform skaters (Figure B), while at stations 2 and 4, the athletes run figure eights. Between stations 1 and 2 and between stations 3 and 4, the athletes perform 10 push-ups. Between stations 2 and 3 and between stations 4 and 1, the athletes perform 30 speed squats (i.e., squat as quickly as possible, but only until the thighs are parallel to the ground). One team begins at station 1 (the first group of cones) and the other team begins at station 3. At the whistle, the athletes perform the desired tasks as quickly as possible. The goal is to catch or overrun the other team, which is accomplished by racing through the cones and performing the calisthenics more quickly than the opponents. The team that is caught loses.

Variations:

- Use medicine ball drills (e.g., chest pass, overhead toss) in place of the calisthenics.

- Use agility ladders in conjunction with, or in place of, the cones.

- Divide the athletes into teams and select an athlete from one team to race an athlete from the opposing team (the winning team picks).

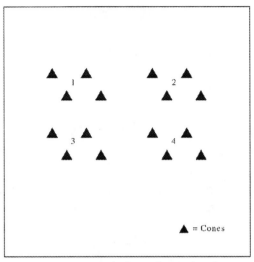

Figure A. Set-up and player formation for Catch Us if You Can

Figure B. Athlete performing skaters

#8: Chuck It

Skills Developed: Aerobic/anaerobic conditioning, agility, manipulative skills, reaction, and speed

Players: 2 or more

Playing Area: Large open area (preferably a gymnasium)

Materials Needed: 12 tennis balls or racquetballs, 1 stopwatch

Description: After you divide the athletes into two equal teams, each team takes possession of half of the playing area and faces the center line. At the whistle, randomly toss six balls on each side of the playing area. The object of the game is for the teams to get rid of all of the balls on their side by throwing them across the center line to the opposing team's side of the playing area. The game lasts approximately one to two minutes. When the allotted time has passed, each team then counts the number of balls on its side. The team in possession of fewer balls at the end of the game wins.

Note:

- Any athlete who throws a ball at another athlete has five penalty points added to his team's score at the end of the game.

Variation:

- Include medicine balls of various weights and add one point per pound/ kilogram to the final score of the team that has the ball on their side of the playing area at the end of the game.

#9: Circle Dodgeball

Skills Developed: Agility, coordination, reaction, and speed

Players: 10–15

Playing Area: Large open area (preferably a gymnasium)

Materials Needed: 1 foam ball, 1 stopwatch

Description: Instruct the athletes to form a large circle with one athlete designated as the dodger (see figure). At the whistle, the timer is started and the athletes in the circle throw the foam ball in an attempt to hit the dodger. Once the dodger has been hit with the ball, he rotates back to his position in the circle, while the athlete directly to his left rotates to the center. If the center athlete catches the ball, he may choose to remain in the center or rotate back to the circle. This game should be continued until each athlete has gone once. The dodger who remains in the center of the circle without being hit for the longest period of time wins.

Note:

- A 10-second penalty should be given to any athlete who hits a dodger with a ball above the neck.

Player formation for Circle Dodgeball

#10: Crab Soccer

Skills Developed: Manipulative skills, muscular strength/endurance, and stability

Players: 8 or more

Playing Area: Large open area (preferably a gymnasium)

Materials Needed: 4 cones/markers, 2 or 3 Swiss balls, soccer balls, or beach balls

Description: Begin by placing the game balls in the center of the playing area and then instruct each team to assume the crab position (see figure) on its goal line. At the whistle, each team performs a crab walk toward the center of the playing area and attempts to kick the balls into the opposing team's goal. One point is awarded for each time an athlete kicks a ball between the designated markers at the opponent's goal line. After a goal is scored, both teams return to their own goal lines and the balls are positioned back in the center of the playing area before the game can resume.

Note:

- Any time a ball is kicked out-of-bounds, the athlete who retrieves the ball should return it to the center of the playing area for the ball to be considered back in play.

Variation:

- If an athlete's rear end should touch the ground at any time during the game (excluding the goalies), you can require that athlete to stop where he is and perform a designated number of push-ups, sit-ups, etc., before being able to return to play.

Crab position

#11: Crossfire

Skills Developed: Aerobic/anaerobic conditioning, agility, balance, coordination, and reaction

Players: 3 or more

Playing Area: Open area (15-feet x 15-feet square or 20-feet x 20-feet square)

Materials Needed: Soft foam/rubber ball

Description: Position two athletes, who serve as throwers, so that they face each other approximately 15 to 20 feet apart. Position a third athlete, who serves as a dodger, in the middle of the two throwers. At the whistle, the throwers throw the ball in an attempt to hit the dodger below the neck. If the dodger is hit, he switches places with the thrower who hit him, and the thrower becomes the new dodger.

Variations:

- Use different size balls.

- Use a larger or smaller square.

- Designate more throwers and/or dodgers.

#12: Dirty Dozen Relay

Skills Developed: Aerobic/anaerobic conditioning and muscular strength/endurance

Players: 2 or more

Playing Area: Large open area

Materials Needed: None

Description: Athletes begin by positioning themselves at either end of the playing area on a predetermined boundary line. At the whistle, each athlete performs one push-up and then jogs to the line at the opposite end of the playing area, only to turn around and return to the starting point and perform two push-ups. Each time the athlete returns to the starting line, another push-up is added until the athlete reaches 12. The first athlete to complete this task wins.

Variations:

- Increase the distance traveled by the athletes.

- Incorporate various locomotor skills as athletes travel across the playing area (e.g., lateral shuffles, backpedaling, carioca).

- Require athletes to transport medicine balls or sand bags from one end of the playing area to the other.

- At one end of the playing area, require another strength-training exercise, such as squats.

- Require athletes to lunge to a predetermined line and then jog the remainder of the distance.

- Divide the athletes into teams and perform this game as a team relay.

#13: Dodge Basketball

Skills Developed: Aerobic/anaerobic conditioning, agility, coordination, reaction, and teamwork

Players: 8 or more

Playing Area: Basketball court

Materials Needed: 1 basketball and 2–4 foam balls

Description: The rules of this game are the same as basketball, with one major exception. Both teams have one or two sideline athletes with at least one foam ball each. The object of the game is for an athlete to shoot and score as many baskets as possible while avoiding being hit by a foam ball thrown by the opposition's sideline athletes. If an athlete shooting baskets is hit by a sideline athlete, then he must jog off the playing area and perform a specific task (e.g., push-ups, squats, jog the court, lunges) Once the athlete has performed this task, he is allowed back in the game.

#14: Drag Race

Skills Developed: Muscular strength/endurance and power

Playing Area: Large open area (preferably a gymnasium)

Materials Needed: Old blankets or sheets (depending on number of athletes involved)

Players: 4 or more

Description: Divide the athletes into teams of two or three players each. Each team is given one blanket or sheet for an athlete to sit on (see figure). The object of the game is to drag the athlete on the blanket/sheet across the playing area and back to the starting line faster than the opposing teams. When the starting line is reached, the athletes switch places and repeat this process until all athletes have had a chance to both drag and be dragged on the blanket or sheet. The game is over when the last team member crosses the starting line. The team to complete this task in the shortest amount of time wins.

Variation:

- Increase the number of athletes being pulled on the blankets.

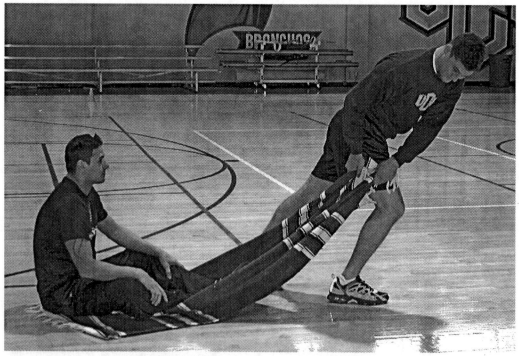

Athlete performing the Drag Race

Athlete performing the farmer's walk with a heavy bag

#15: Dragon's Treasure

Skills Developed: Aerobic/anaerobic conditioning, agility, and reaction

Players: 8 or more

Playing Area: Large open area

Materials Needed: 4 hula hoops, 20 bean bags or balls, and 1 jump rope

Description: Prepare for this game by doing the following: position one hula hoop in the center of the playing area and scatter the other three hula hoops around the playing area at an equal distance from the center hula hoop (see figure). Then, place 20 bean bags in the center hula hoop. Before dividing the athletes into three teams of treasure hunters, select one athlete to be the dragon and another to be the keeper. The dragon and keeper each hold one end of the jump rope and station themselves at the center hula hoop. The keeper must stand next to the hula hoop, where he is only aloud to pivot. The dragon is able to move freely within the range of the rope. After dividing the athletes into three teams, designate a hula hoop for each team. At the whistle, the athletes, or treasure hunters, attempt to steal the treasure (i.e., the bean bags) from the dragon's hoard. The dragon's job is to stop the hunters by tagging them. If a treasure hunter manages to steal treasure from the dragon's hoard, then he must put it in his team's hula hoop. However, if the treasure hunter is tagged by the dragon in the process, then he must put the treasure back where he found it and perform 10 bodyweight squats, push-ups, etc., before reentering the game. The game continues until time is up (five to 10 minutes), or until all the treasure has been stolen. The team with the most treasure wins.

Variations:

- Use weighted objects in place of the bean bags (e.g., light dumbbells, medicine balls).

- Instruct the dragon and/or athletes to hop on one foot.

- Use a longer or shorter rope.

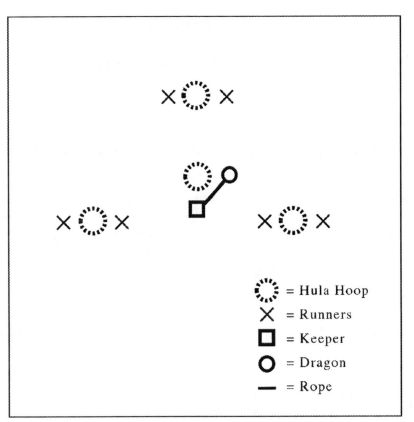

Set-up and player formation for Dragon's Treasure

#16: Eagle Walk

Skills Developed: Coordination, flexibility, muscular strength, and endurance

Players: 1 or more

Playing Area: Open area

Materials Needed: 4-foot-long dowel rods or PVC pipes (the quantity depends on the number of athletes)

Description: This game can be played for time or against another athlete. Each athlete grabs a dowel rod, steps behind the starting line, and assumes an overhead squat position with the thighs approximately parallel to the floor (see figure). On the whistle, the athletes race for approximately 60 feet while walking on their heels and maintaining at least a three-quarter squat position.

Note:

- Do not allow athletes to let their knees travel in front of their toes during the game.

Variations:

- If only one athlete is available, have him perform a timed trial and then allow two additional trials to compare best times.

- For large groups, this game can be performed in a relay.

- Instead of dowel rods, athletes may use dumbbells, weighted bars, or medicine balls.

- Once the athlete crosses a predetermined point, instruct him to perform an overhead press and then return the bar to an overhead squat position before returning to the starting line.

Overhead squat position

#17: Elimination

Skills Developed: Agility, reaction, and speed

Players: 8 or more

Playing Area: Volleyball court

Materials Needed: 1 volleyball

Description: After dividing the athletes into two equal teams, instruct each team to gather on their side of the playing area and spread out in a random pattern. At this point, flip a coin to determine which team is to put the ball into play first. The object of the game is to throw the ball over the net into an area where the opposing team is unlikely to catch it. When the ball is dropped or missed, the athlete closest to the ball is eliminated. Eliminated athletes must then jog around the playing area until the last remaining athlete is declared the winner.

Notes:

- Athletes may take only two steps from the point at which they receive the ball. If more than two steps are taken, then that athlete is eliminated.

- After an athlete is eliminated, the team that loses its athlete gains possession of the ball.

#18: End Zone Ball

Skills Developed: Aerobic/anaerobic conditioning, agility, and speed

Players: 8 or more

Playing Area: Large open area (preferably a gymnasium or basketball court)

Materials Needed: 2–4 volleyballs, basketballs, or footballs

Description: Divide the athletes equally into two teams and designate a third of each team as receivers and the other two-thirds as guards (see figure). The object of the game is for the guards to throw the ball over the heads of the opposing team's guards to their own receivers while trying to prevent the opposing team's receivers from catching balls thrown by their guards. All the guards must remain on their side of the playing area, and each end-zone athlete must remain in the end zone. One point is awarded for each ball successfully caught in the end zone by an end-zone athlete. The team with the most points at the close of the game wins.

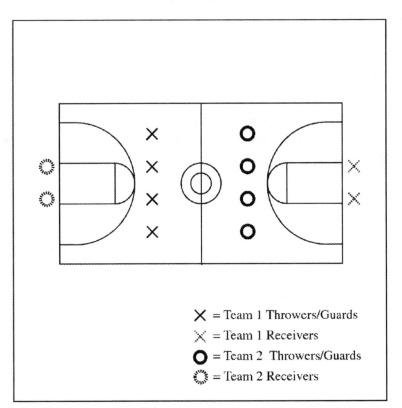

X = Team 1 Throwers/Guards
X = Team 1 Receivers
O = Team 2 Throwers/Guards
O = Team 2 Receivers

Player formation for End Zone Ball

#19: Everybody's It

Skills Developed: Agility, reaction, and speed

Players: 4 or more

Playing area: Large open area

Materials Needed: None

Description: This game is played just like tag except everyone is "it." Athletes spread out randomly over the playing area and await the whistle blow. The object of the game is to tag as many athletes as possible without being tagged in the process. If an athlete is tagged, then that athlete must immediately drop to the ground and perform five push-ups before rejoining the game.

Note:

- If a dispute arises about which athlete was tagged first, then both athletes must perform push-ups.

Variations:

- Require athletes to perform other conditioning exercises after being tagged (e.g., squats, lunges, down-ups).

- Have an elimination round. If an athlete is tagged, then he must move to the sideline and perform conditioning drills, such as jogging in place or jumping jacks, until only one athlete remains.

#20: Fill 'er Up

Skills Developed: Aerobic/anaerobic conditioning and muscular strength/endurance

Players: 4 or more

Playing Area: Large open area

Materials Needed: Assortment of light and heavy objects (e.g., medicine balls, footballs, sandbags), and 2 bags large enough to hold all the objects

Description: After dividing the athletes into two equal teams, divide the objects equally (one per athlete) into separate piles five feet in front and to the left of the first athlete in line (see figure). Position each bag 10 yards from the starting line. At the whistle, the first athlete runs and picks up an object, sprints to the bag, places the object inside the bag, and then sprints back to tag the next athlete in line. The athlete carrying the last object places it in the bag and then sprints back, dragging the bag behind him. The first team to drag the bag past the starting line wins.

Variations:

- Adjust the distance to the first object and/or the bag.

- Instruct each athlete to perform the game using a different motor skill (e.g., hop on one foot).

- Increase or decrease the number of objects used.

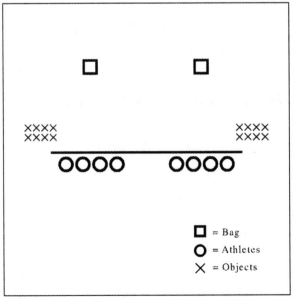

Set-up and player formation for Fill 'er Up

#21: Fill the Bucket

Skills Developed: Aerobic/anaerobic conditioning and muscular strength/endurance

Players: 6 or more

Playing Area: Large open area

Materials Needed: Tennis balls and buckets (quantity needed is based on the number of athletes)

Description: Divide the athletes into two to four teams, depending on the number of athletes. Set up a bucket and six tennis balls approximately 10 yards in front of each team. At the whistle, the first athlete runs down and performs six push-ups. However, during the upward phase of each push-up, the athlete drops one tennis ball into the bucket. The athlete alternates hands after each drop. After completing six push-ups, the athlete dumps out the balls and sprints 10 yards to tag the next athlete in line. Meanwhile, the other athletes must perform different exercises while waiting to be tagged. Depending on the size of the group, you can designate each spot in line to correspond with a different exercise. For example, if four athletes are on each team, one athlete is performing the relay (push-ups), the next athlete can be holding a squat position, the third athlete can be performing jumping jacks, and the fourth athlete can be performing lunges. This cycle continues until all of the athletes have completed the push-up relay along with their designated exercises while waiting in line. The first team to complete this task is the winner.

Variations:

- Adjust the distance between the starting line and the bucket (e.g., 20 yards).

- Instruct the athletes to pick up sandbags and position them in a trash can, in which case the athletes should perform squats rather than push-ups during the relay.

- Place different objects in the bucket (e.g., bricks, water balloons, sandbags)

#22: Fireman Relay

Skills Developed: Aerobic/anaerobic conditioning, balance, strength, and teamwork

Players: 4 or more

Playing Area: Open area

Materials Needed: 2 cones or markers

Description: Divide the athletes equally into two to four teams. Position the cones/markers 40 yards apart to indicate the starting line and the relay station. At the whistle, the first athletes in line picks up the next athlete in line and positions him over his shoulders (see figure). The first athlete carries his teammate 40 yards to the relay station, switches roles with that teammate, then returns to the starting line. The first team to cross the finish line with all of its athletes wins. If the teams include an odd number of athletes, use a 20-yard playing area and require the athletes to make a complete pass (i.e., around the cone and back). The athlete who is carried serves as the new carrier, and the next athlete in line is carried.

Variations:

*   Pair up the athletes and have them carry each other for distance. The team that carries each other the farthest wins.

*   Instruct the athletes to walk in figure-eight patterns around cones that have been spread out between the starting line and relay station.

Athlete performing a fireman carry

#23: Fistball

Skills Developed: Aerobic/anaerobic conditioning, agility, manipulative skills, and reaction

Players: 2–4

Playing Area: An unobstructed wall or hard surface with two boundary lines marked approximately 10–12 feet apart and a serving line 5 feet from the wall (see figure). This game is best played in a gymnasium or on a racquetball court.

Materials Needed: 1 playground ball approximately 7 to 12 inches in diameter

Description: This game begins with an athlete serving the ball with a closed fist so that it travels across the serve line, first striking the ground, then the wall (though the ball does not necessarily need to bounce over the serving line on the return). Once the ball is in play, the game continues, with the ball always hitting ground-wall-ground. When the nonserving athlete misses the ball or hits it out of bounds, a point is given to the serving athlete. If the serving athlete misses the ball or hits it out of bounds, his opponent then becomes the server. Points may only be scored by the serving athlete.

Variations:

*   Athletes can play to a predetermined score.

*   Athletes can play for time.

*   You may substitute the playground ball with a medicine ball. Instead of hitting it, the athletes can catch and throw the ball, with the ball always hitting ground-wall-ground.

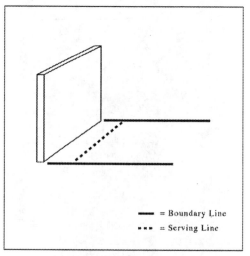

——— = Boundary Line

• • • = Serving Line

Proper set-up for Fistball

#24: Flamingo Pass

Skills Developed: Aerobic/anaerobic conditioning, agility, balance, coordination, muscular strength/endurance, power, and reaction

Players: 6–12

Playing Area: Open area

Materials Needed: Medicine ball

Description: Divide the athletes into teams and ask them to select one athlete to be the mobile athlete. Instruct the stationary athletes on each team to line up side-by-side and approximately five feet apart. The mobile athlete then faces his teammates at least six to eight feet in front of the opposing team's athletes. On the whistle, the mobile athlete stands across from the first stationary teammate. The mobile athlete and his teammate then pass the medicine ball back and forth five times while standing on their left foot. If either athlete drops the ball or touches the ground with his right foot, the count starts over. After five successful passes, the mobile athlete hops to the next teammate and repeats the process. When the mobile athlete reaches the end, he switches feet and repeats the process with each of his teammates. The team that goes down and back first wins. All athletes must remain standing on one foot at all times.

Variations:

- Adjust the distance between the athletes (a closer distance equals a faster pace, whereas a longer distance requires more strength and power and creates a slower pace).

- Time one team and then have the opposing team attempt to beat that time.

- Change the object being thrown (e.g., football, racquetball, sandbag).

- Require the stationary athletes to perform various conditioning exercises while waiting for their turns (e.g., squats, jumping jacks).

- An athlete performing a chest pass in the Flamingo stance

#25: Flip the Bear

Skills Developed: Power, strength, and stability

Players: 2 athletes of equal size and ability

Playing Area: Open area free of clutter

Materials Needed: 1 large floor mat (6 feet x 6 feet or larger)

Description: This game begins with one athlete, the bear, kneeling on all-fours, while another athlete assumes a position on his knees beside the bear (see figure). At the whistle, the athlete on his knees grabs the bear and attempts to flip him over onto his back. Punching and kicking is strictly prohibited. Once the bear has been flipped, the athletes switch roles and repeat.

Player positions for Flip the Bear

#26: Floor Touch Wrestle

Skills Developed: Muscular strength/endurance, power, and stability

Players: 2 athletes of equal size and ability

Playing Area: Small open area

Materials Needed: None

Description: Two athletes begin by grasping each other's right hands while simultaneously positioning themselves in a staggered stance with the left foot leading. At the whistle, each athlete attempts to make his opponent touch the ground with the back of his hand (see figure). Once this task has been accomplished, the athletes switch feet and hands and repeat.

Floor touch wrestle

#27: Free for All

Skills Developed: Aerobic/anaerobic conditioning, agility, balance, coordination, and reaction

Players: 10 or more

Playing Area: Large open area (preferably an indoor court)

Materials Needed: 3 soft foam/rubber balls

Description: The rules for this game are similar to dodgeball. However, rather than forming teams, each athlete fends for himself. Position the three balls in the center of the playing area and instruct the athletes to lie on their stomachs along the baselines. At the whistle, the athletes get up and run toward the balls. At this point, each athlete attempts to retrieve a ball and throw it at another athlete. The goal is to be the last athlete standing.

Notes:

- Athletes may only handle one ball at a time (even when only two athletes remain in the game).

- If the ball is caught or hits an athlete in the head, the thrower is eliminated.

- Athletes who are eliminated should run laps until the next game begins.

Variations:

- Increase or decrease the number of balls in play.

- Rather than having the eliminated athletes run laps, instruct them to perform 10 push-ups and then rejoin the game.

- The athletes can play for an allotted amount of time.

- Set up two games simultaneously. When an athlete is eliminated, he can join the other game in progress.

#28: Gauntlet

Skills Developed: Aerobic/anaerobic conditioning, agility, and reaction

Players: 12 or more

Playing Area: Large open area

Materials Needed: 3–5 soft foam/rubber balls and 4–8 cones/markers

Description: Using the cones, make two 30-yard-long lines parallel to each other and approximately 10 to 15 feet apart (see figure). Then, choose two to four athletes, or throwers (depending on group size), to stand on the lines facing each other, with those on one side of the line holding the balls. The goal of the athletes who are not standing on either line is to run through the gauntlet without being hit. These athletes, the runners, are allowed to backpedal, duck, jump, drop, roll, or do whatever it takes to reach the other side without being hit by a ball. When an athlete is hit, he becomes an additional thrower. The athletes who make it through the gauntlet without being hit can elect to choose a "challenge" for the throwers (e.g., 10 push-ups). The athletes should repeat this process until all of the athletes have served as runners and throwers.

Variations:

- Use a wider or narrower course.

- Use a variety of balls (i.e., larger and smaller).

- Instruct the throwers to use only their nondominant arm to throw the ball.

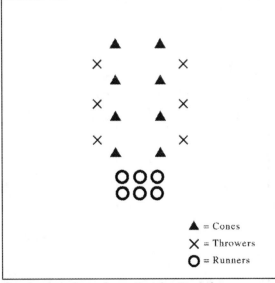

Set-up and player formation for Gauntlet

#29: Heads or Tails

Skills Developed: Aerobic/anaerobic conditioning, agility, and reaction

Players: 4 or more

Playing Area: Large open area

Materials Needed: 1 quarter and 4–8 cones/markers

Description: Divide the athletes into two teams of equal skill (e.g., do not put all of the linemen on one team and the receivers on the other). Name the teams either heads or tails. Before play begins, use the cones to mark two center lines parallel to each other and approximately six feet apart. Next, mark two scoring zones 20 yards from each center line (see figure). To begin, instruct each team to stand along a separate center line with their backs facing the backs of their opponents (i.e., the teams are facing their scoring zone). Next, flip the coin. When the coin lands, yell either "heads" or "tails." The team whose name is called tries to sprint to its scoring zone before being tagged by the opposing team. Points are given for each athlete who makes it across to his scoring zone. This process is repeated until both teams have gone an equal number of times. If needed, you can randomly call out "heads" or "tails" to allow for an equal number of attempts to score.

Variations:

- Require athletes to face each other on the center line.

- Reduce the distance between the center lines (e.g., three feet).

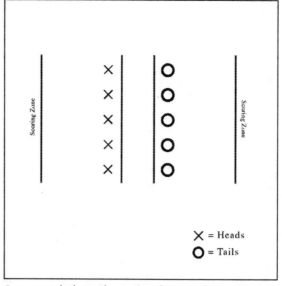

Set-up and player formation for Heads or Tails

#30: Hit 'n' Run

Skills Developed: Anaerobic conditioning and reaction

Players: 2 or more

Playing Area: Large open area

Materials Needed: 2 cones, 1 bat, 1 ball (i.e., Wiffle® ball)

Description: Set the cones up approximately 10 to 15 yards apart. The batter stands near one cone and the fielder stands approximately 40 feet from the batter and pitches the ball. The batter scores points by sprinting from cone to cone after hitting the ball (with each cone valued at an increasing number of points). The fielder must retrieve the ball as quickly as possible and tag the batter to stop points from being scored.

Variations:

- Implement baseball rules (e.g., strikes, balls, outs).

- Use different types of bats (e.g., tennis racket, broom stick).

- Use different types of balls (e.g., football, reaction ball).

#31: Hole in One

Skills Developed: Muscular strength/endurance and teamwork

Players: 8 or more

Playing Area: Large open area

Materials Needed: 4–8 medicine balls (or heavy objects), 4 hula hoops (secured with stakes, a heavy object, or an athlete), 4 cones/markers

Description: Position the cones in a straight line with 10 feet between each and then position a hula hoop 10 to 15 feet in front of each cone (see figure). Divide the athletes into four teams, give each team one or two medicine balls, and then instruct each team to stand behind a cone. At the whistle, the first athlete on each team uses a chest pass to attempt to throw a medicine ball into the hula hoop. The team receives one point for each successful throw. Once an athlete has scored two points for his team, the next athlete in line throws. This process continues until all of a team's athletes have scored two points and the first team to do so wins.

Variations:

- Designate a particular throw (e.g., overhead, underhand, rotational, backward).

- Instruct the athletes to play for a certain amount of time, and the team with the most points at the end of that time wins.

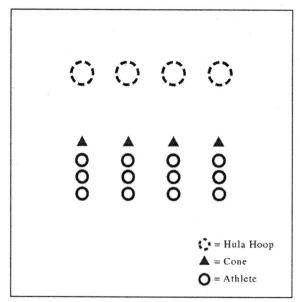

Set-up and player formation for Hole in One

#32: Hop Tag

Skills Developed: Aerobic/anaerobic conditioning, muscular strength/endurance, and power

Players: 4 or more

Playing Area: Large open area

Materials Needed: None

Description: Designate one athlete as the initial tagger to start the game. That athlete, while hopping on two feet, attempts to tag the other athletes, who are also hopping on two feet. As soon as the initial tagger is able to tag another athlete, that athlete becomes the new tagger and pursues the other athletes in the same manner.

Variation:

• Increase the intensity by having the athletes perform the game while hopping on one leg (switching legs after a predetermined period of time).

#33: Hot Ball

Skills Developed: Aerobic/anaerobic conditioning, balance, coordination, muscular strength/endurance, and reaction

Players: 6 or more

Playing Area: Large open area

Materials Needed: 1 medicine ball (weight based on the strength of the athletes)

Description: The rules of this game are very similar to the classic game of hot potato, the only variation being that the "potato" is a heavier and more cumbersome object. Instruct the athletes to stand in a circle with approximately two feet separating them. At the whistle, the athletes begin to pass the medicine ball back and forth to any other player they choose until you blow the whistle again (every 20 seconds). However, every player must be passed the ball before an athlete is allowed to pass it back to any athlete a second time. The athlete holding the medicine ball at the sound of the second whistle is eliminated and must run laps until the next round is completed. At the next whistle, the runners perform push-ups, sit-ups, and so on until the game is over. The athletes remaining in the circle continue to play until only one athlete remains. The last athlete standing wins and does not have to perform the running/push-up routine.

Variation:

- Introduce another ball into the circle (preferably of a different weight than the ball already in play).

#34: I Got Your Number

Skills Developed: Anaerobic conditioning, agility, balance, coordination, and reaction

Players: 12 or more

Playing Area: Large open area

Materials Needed: 2 soft foam/rubber balls

Description: Divide the athletes equally into two teams and have each team secretly assign sequential numbers to each of its athletes (starting with the number one). Once the numbers have been assigned, have all of the athletes form a large circle with a line down the middle dividing the teams (the athletes do not have to be in sequential order). Then, position a ball on each side of the line. To begin, you or the "odd man out" should call out a number. When a number is called, both athletes who have been assigned that number must run out, try to grab the ball, and be first to hit the opposing athlete of the same number with the ball. The first athlete to do so scores a point. Balls that are blocked or caught by an opponent are considered out of play, and that opponent has a chance to score by throwing a ball at the athlete who has already thrown. The first team to score 10 points wins. After each one-on-one session, the balls are left where the last athletes dropped them (with one ball remaining on each side).

Variations:

- Assign two different numbers to each athlete. In this variation, one or two athletes should step out when a number is called.

- Allow two balls in play on each side of the playing area and require two hits to score one point.

- Position one ball in the center of the circle and have the athletes sprint to the ball. If the ball is caught by the other athlete, then the thrower loses a point or the catcher receives a point.

- Require the stationary athletes to perform various conditioning exercises while waiting for their turns (e.g., squats, jumping jacks).

#35: In the Zone

Skills Developed: Aerobic/anaerobic conditioning, agility, balance, coordination, muscular strength/endurance, and power

Players: 8–12

Playing Area: Football field or large open area

Materials Needed: 2 sets of heavy dumbbells/bumper plates (size based on the size and strength of the athletes), 2 agility ladders, 10 cones

Description: This game is physically demanding for most athletes. Divide the athletes equally into teams (based on speed and strength). Position the dumbbells at the 10-yard line, the ladder at the 30-yard line, and the cones at the 60-yard line in a zigzag pattern (Figure A). At the whistle, the first athlete sprints to the 10-yard line, picks up the dumbbells/bumper plates, and performs a 20-yard farmer's walk (Figure B) to the starting line and then back to the 10-yard line. Once the athlete is back to the 10-yard line, he sets the weights down and sprints to the agility ladder. He then sprints through the ladder while performing the various drills or other appropriate skills that you've designated. Once through the ladder, the athlete sprints to the cones and weaves through them. Upon reaching the last cone, the athlete sprints to the other end zone. Meanwhile, the next athlete in line begins the relay as soon as the athlete in front of him has set down the dumbbells. The relay continues until all of the athletes have completed the run. The team to finish first wins.

Note:

- Once an athlete reaches the end zone, instruct him to walk or jog slowly before resting (i.e., do not let the athlete lie on the ground after completing the relay).

Variations:

- Adjust the length of the field.

- Instruct the athletes to perform a fireman's carry or sandbag drag (or a combination) rather than a farmer's walk.

- Instruct the athletes to remain at each station until they are tagged by the next athlete.

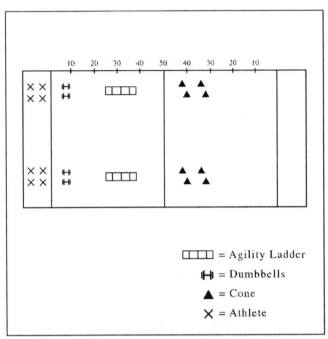

Figure A. Set-up and player formation for In the Zone

Figure B. Farmer's walk

#36: Invade and Conquer

Skills Developed: Aerobic/anaerobic conditioning and agility

Players: 8 or more

Playing Area: Large playing area

Materials Needed: 8 hula hoops/cones, 4 balls, 4 different colored shirts (optional)

Description: To prepare, divide the playing area into four sections with clearly defined boundaries and then position one hula hoop and one ball at the far corner of each section. Then, position the other hula hoops near the sidelines, outside of the playing area (see figure). This area serves as the holding area for tagged athletes. Each team should have their own designated holding area. Then, divide the athletes into four teams wearing different colored shirts (optional). At the whistle, each team attempts to retrieve the other teams' balls and place them in its own hula hoop. If an athlete is tagged while in another section, then that athlete must go to the holding area until a teammate helps him out by running into the opposing team's territory and tagging him. The game continues until all four balls are in one team's territory.

Variations:

- The athletes can play for time, and the team with the most balls in its territory when time runs out wins.

- Allow the teams to "recruit" teammates by stealing them out of another territory's holding area.

- Use medicine balls or heavy objects instead of lighter balls.

- Once in the holding area, the athletes can perform calisthenics until the game has ended.

- The team with the most balls or captured athletes in its holding area wins (after a designated amount of time).

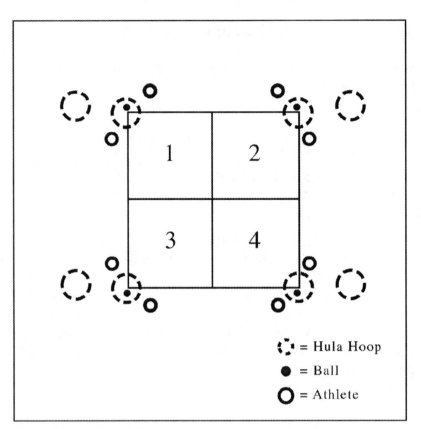

Set-up for Invade and Conquer

#37: Jigsaw Relay

Skills Developed: Aerobic/anaerobic conditioning, agility, cognitive ability, coordination, reaction, and teamwork

Players: 8 or more

Playing Area: Large open area

Materials Needed: 2 puzzles (10–25 pieces each), 1 table or board (large enough for the puzzle), as well as multiple cones, agility ladders, and hurdles (i.e., obstacle course materials)

Description: Set up two identical obstacle courses next to each another that span 30 to 40 yards (see figure). Then, position the puzzle boxes (without the picture) 10 feet from the starting line. At the end of each obstacle course, set up a table where the puzzle will be constructed. Once preparation is complete, divide the athletes equally into two teams and instruct them to line up behind the starting line. At the whistle, the first athlete in line sprints to the puzzle box, grabs a single piece, and then sprints through the obstacle course. Upon finishing, the athlete sets the piece on the table and sprints back to tag the next teammate in line. This process repeats until one team completes the puzzle.

Note:

- One strategy is for the athletes to start with the borders and build in. However, the primary strategies should be outlined by the teams themselves.

Variations:

- Allow the athletes to see the picture of the puzzle before beginning the relay.

- Allow 60 seconds for the athletes to develop a strategy for efficiently completing the puzzle.

- A similar option is to position the tables at the starting line, where teams can work on putting the puzzle together while one athlete from each team is out sprinting for another piece.

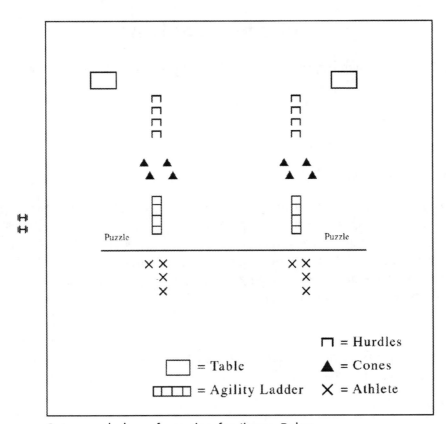

Puzzle · Puzzle

= Hurdles
= Table
= Cones
= Agility Ladder
= Athlete

Set-up and player formation for Jigsaw Relay

#38: Junk Yard Wars

Skills Developed: Aerobic/anaerobic conditioning, agility, balance, coordination, and reaction

Players: 4 or more

Playing Area: Large open area

Materials Needed: Several old car/truck tires

Description: Scatter the tires anywhere from two to six feet apart in a large playing area and instruct each athlete to stand on a tire (one athlete per tire). At the whistle, the athletes jump from tire to tire in an attempt to knock other athletes off of their tires. If an athlete is knocked off a tire, he must run three laps around the tires. Once the laps are completed, the athlete rejoins the game by jumping onto an unoccupied tire. The athlete who runs the fewest laps wins.

Note:

- Do not run this game if the tires are wet, as they may become slick and increase the chances of injury.

Variation:

- Give each athlete two flags and instruct him to put the flags in his side pockets. The objective of this variation is for athletes to remove the flags from the pockets of opposing athletes. If an athlete loses his flags, he must run laps until another game begins. The athlete with the most flags wins.

#39: Kickboard Relay

Skills Developed: Aerobic/anaerobic conditioning, balance, coordination, and muscular strength/endurance

Players: 8 or more

Playing Area: Swimming pool

Materials Needed: 2–4 kickboards

Description: Divide the athletes equally into two teams and instruct half of each team to go to opposite ends of the swimming pool with a kickboard (see figure). At the whistle, the first athletes in line swim across the pool using the kickboards. Upon reaching the opposite end, the athletes hand off their kickboards to the next athletes in line. After receiving the kickboard, those athletes swim to the opposite end of the swimming pool. This process is repeated until all of the athletes have switched sides of the pool. The first team to complete this task wins.

Notes:

- A lifeguard is required for this activity.

- Players that are unable to swim should be given an alternative activity.

Variations:

- Require the athletes to swim down and back before handing off the their kickboards.

- Require the athletes to tread water while waiting in line.

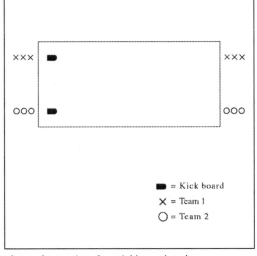

Player formation for Kickboard Relay

#40: King Crab

Skills Developed: Muscular strength/endurance, power, and stability

Players: 2–3

Playing Area: Large open area

Materials Needed: Masking tape

Description: Begin by marking a six-feet by six-feet playing area with masking tape and instruct both athletes to assume a crab position (Figure A) in the center of the square with their backs against each another. At the whistle, the athletes attempt to push each other out of the designated playing area.

Variation:

- Add a third athlete to make the game more challenging (Figure B). Once one athlete is eliminated by crossing the tape line, the remaining two athletes return to the center of the ring and compete against each other.

Figure A. Two-player King Crab formation

Figure B. Three-player King Crab formation

#41: King of the Mountain Tug-of-War

Skills Developed: Balance, muscular strength/endurance, power, and stability

Players: 2–4

Playing Area: Large open area

Materials Needed: 1–4 small ropes/resistance chords, 2–4 balance discs

Description: While standing on a balance disc, each athlete shares a rope or resistance chord with at least one other athlete (Figure A). At the whistle, the athletes must try to maintain their balance on top of their discs while trying to pull their opponents off balance using the rope or resistance chord. The athlete who remains on the balance apparatus the longest wins.

Variation:

- The athletes can stand on one leg (Figure B). Instruct the athletes to perform this game while alternating between standing on their right and left legs.

Figure A. Three-player formation

Figure B. Single-leg variation

#42: Knee Slaps

Skill Developed: Reaction

Players: 2

Playing Area: Open area

Materials Needed: 4–8 cones/markers

Description: Begin by positioning the cones/markers in a 6 feet by 6 feet square to delineate the boundaries for this game. The athletes assume a staggered stance and face each other from approximately three feet apart in the center of the square. At the whistle, both athletes attempt to lean forward and slap their opponent's knees without being slapped in the process (see figure). Athletes may dodge and block as needed to avoid being slapped. The first athlete to win two matches is declared the winner.

Note:

*   The athletes should be approximately the same size and possess roughly the same amount of strength.

Variations:

*   The athletes can play for a specific amount of time.

*   The athletes can play to a higher number of touches (e.g., 10).

Players attempting to tag their opponent's knees

#43: Land Mine

Skills Developed: Agility, muscular strength/endurance, and power

Players: 2 or more

Playing Area: Large open area

Materials Needed: 10 cones/markers

Description: Instruct the athletes to form a large circle and grasp the wrists of both athletes next to them. If only two athletes are competing, they should face each other while grasping each other's right/left wrist. Next, randomly place cones inside the designated playing area. At the whistle, each athlete will push or pull an opposing athlete in an attempt to force him to touch or knock over a cone. Any athlete who touches a cone is eliminated from the game. Also, if any athlete breaks his grip during the competition, he is eliminated from the game.

Variation:

•   Instruct the athletes to perform the game while hopping on one leg.

#44: Launch Pad

Skills Developed: Agility, balance, coordination, muscular strength/endurance, reaction, and teamwork

Players: 4 or more

Playing Area: Large open area

Materials Needed: At least 2 large towels, medicine balls

Description: Instruct two sets of athletes to hold the ends of a towel. One set of athletes starts with a medicine ball in the middle of its towel. The goal is to launch the medicine ball toward the other set of athletes (see figure), and for that set of athletes to catch the medicine ball using its towel. The first set of athletes to drop the medicine ball loses.

Variations:

- The athletes can use water balloons in place of medicine balls.

- Specify boundaries and distances from which the ball must be thrown to qualify for points.

Medicine ball being prepared for launch

#45: Leap Frog

Skills Developed: Aerobic/anaerobic conditioning, agility, muscular endurance, and reaction

Players: 8 or more

Playing Area: Large open area

Materials Needed: 2 cones

Description: Position two cones approximately 20 yards from each other. The first cone will serve as the starting line and the second cone will be the finish line. Divide the athletes into teams consisting of four or five athletes. Instruct all but one athlete from each team to kneel on the ground with their elbows on the ground and head tucked between their arms (see figure). Each athlete is approximately two feet from his neighbor. At the whistle, the athlete left standing jumps over each athlete individually. When the standing athlete has jumped over the last kneeling athlete, he assumes the same kneeling position as the other athletes. The next athlete at the start of the line (i.e., the athlete who was jumped over first) then stands up and begins jumping over the kneeling athletes in the same manner. This process continues until all of the athletes cross the finish line. The team to cross first wins.

Variations:

- Rather than playing for quickest time, the athletes can play for a set amount of time, so that the team that goes the farthest distance in the set amount of time wins.

- To improve reaction, you can blow a whistle to initiate a change of direction. The jumping athlete changes direction while the kneeling athletes adapt to the change in direction by repositioning themselves accordingly.

Athlete preparing to bound over teammates

#46: Lily Pad

Skills Developed: Balance, strategy, and teamwork

Players: 8 or more

Playing Area: Open area

Materials Needed: Balance disks or boards measuring 2 feet by 4 feet by 2 inches (4 fewer disks or boards than the number of athletes)

Description: Divide the athletes into teams and give each team enough materials for each member minus two (i.e., 10 athletes receive eight "lily pads"). The object of the game is for each team to move its teammates across the designated playing area by using the pads. Each team must come up with a strategy to get its members across the area without touching the ground. The area can be anywhere from five to 10 yards, depending on the number of athletes and individual skill levels. Each team must also come up with a way to pass all the pads back to the next athlete, who still needs to cross the playing area. The first team to successfully move all of its members across the designated area wins.

Variations:

- Use smaller or larger balance equipment for the pads.

- Establish a time limit for each member to cross the playing area.

- Establish a time limit for each team to cross the playing area, so that the team with the most athletes across the playing area at the end of the designated time wins.

- Have the athletes hold a small medicine ball as they cross the playing area.

#47: Load Up

Skills Developed: Aerobic/anaerobic conditioning and muscular strength/endurance

Players: 4 or more

Playing Area: Football field or large open area

Materials Needed: Assortment of heavy objects (e.g., medicine balls, sandbags), 2 sleds (old car hoods work great), and 2 lengths of rope or chain

Description: Randomly place an assortment of heavy objects in a straight line in the playing area. Divide the athletes into two teams and position two heavy objects (one for each team) every 10 yards over a total of 80 yards. Then, tie a large rope or chain to each sled and instruct each team to prepare to drag its sled, starting at 10 yards from the first object. At the whistle, each team drags its sled down the field while collecting heavy objects and placing them on the sled. The athletes take turns lifting the heavy objects onto the sled. When the last object is retrieved, the athletes drag their sleds the last 20 yards as quickly as possible. The first team to cross the finish line wins.

Notes:

- If using a chain, wrap it with cloth or burlap to help protect the athletes' hands. Also, supply the athletes with leather work gloves.

- If using an old car hood, remove all sharp objects that could possibly inflict injury to the athletes or damage equipment.

Variation:

- Vary the weight and size of the objects (e.g., empty 50-gallon barrels, cinder blocks, large rocks).

#48: Medicine Ball Four-Square

Skills Developed: Agility, manipulative skills, power, and reaction

Players: 4

Playing Area: Area measuring 10 feet by 10 feet, divided into 4 equal-sized squares (see figure)

Materials Needed: 1 rubber medicine ball that bounces

Description: Each athlete positions himself in a square labeled 1, 2, 3, or 4. The server (in square 1) puts the medicine ball into play by bouncing it using an underhand serve (palm up) into any of his three opponents' squares. The athlete guarding that square first allows the medicine ball to bounce once, and then quickly propels the medicine ball back into any of the other squares. The object of the game is to eliminate an athlete so that the remaining athletes can rotate squares (counter-numerically) to reach the server's square. For example, if the athlete in square 3 is eliminated, then the athlete in square 3 rotates to square 4, the player in square 4 enters square 3, and the athletes in squares 1 and 2 remain where they are. Play continues until one of the following situations occurs:

- The medicine ball touches any part of the body other than the hands.

- After the serve, an athlete touches the medicine ball before it has bounced.

- The medicine ball bounces more than once in an athlete's square before that athlete can serve the medicine ball to another square.

- A medicine ball hits any line or is thrown out of bounds.

- An athlete serves the medicine ball and it bounces into his own square.

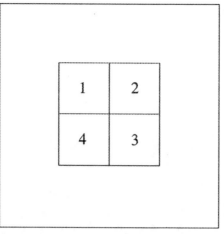

Set-up for Medicine Ball Four-Square

#49: Medicine Ball Hop Relay

Skills Developed: Power and teamwork

Players: 4 or more

Playing Area: Large open area

Materials Needed: 4–6 medicine balls and 2 cones/markers

Description: Divide the athletes equally into four to six teams. The first athlete on each team steps up to the first marker and positions a medicine ball between his knees. At the whistle, the athlete hops to the second marker (approximately 20 to 30 feet from the starting line), and then returns to the first marker (see figure). If the athlete drops or touches the medicine ball with his hands, he must retrieve the medicine ball, run back to the last marker crossed, position the medicine ball back between his knees, and start again. After an athlete crosses both markers, the medicine ball is passed to the next athlete in line, and the process is repeated. The first team to complete the challenge wins.

Variations:

- Increase the distance traveled.

- Instruct the athletes to perform hops forward, laterally, and backward.

- Give two or three medicine balls of various weights to each team, and have the athletes transport each ball across both lines.

Athletes racing toward the finish line

#50: Medicine Ball Run

Skills Developed: Aerobic/anaerobic conditioning, agility, and muscular strength/endurance

Players: 8 or more

Playing Area: Large open area

Materials Needed: 2 medicine balls, 10 cones/markers

Description: Divide the athletes equally into two teams. Next, place the cones approximately 10 to 15 feet apart in two rows and position a medicine ball at the starting line (10 to 15 feet from the first cone). At the whistle, the first athlete from each team zigzags through the cones and returns to the first cone. The athlete then performs a chest pass with the medicine ball to the next athlete in line. Once finished, the runner performs 10 squat thrusts before the next athlete can zigzag through the cones. The first team to successfully complete the course wins. Also, while waiting for their teammate to finish zigzagging through the cones, the athletes waiting in line perform calisthenics. The first athlete in line should perform body-weight squats, which will allow him to maintain eye contact with his teammate before the pass is made. The other athletes can perform a variety of exercises (e.g., push-ups, sit-ups, squat thrusts).

Variations:

- Use a football and instruct the athletes to successfully complete a pass before the next athlete can begin.

- Use an agility ladder and/or hurdles along with the cones to make the course longer and more difficult.

- Instruct the athletes to dribble a soccer ball through the course. This game can be used with soccer and nonsoccer athletes.

#51: Medicine Ball Speed Throw

Skills Developed: Muscular strength/endurance, power, reaction, speed, and teamwork

Players: 2 or more

Playing Area: Large open area

Materials Needed: Medicine balls (dependent on number of athletes) and a stopwatch.

Description: Begin by pairing up the athletes. Next, position the athletes so they are facing each other approximately 10 feet apart. Utilizing a basic chest pass, each pair of athletes performs as many passes with the medicine ball as possible in 30 seconds. The athletes are responsible for keeping track of the number of completed passes.

Notes:

- Athletes should be paired with individuals of like size, strength, and ability.

- When selecting a medicine ball, try to assign medicine balls that are approximately 5 percent of the athlete's bodyweight. For example, if the two athletes are approximately 200 pounds, they should use a 10-pound medicine ball.

Variation:

- Use various throws, such as an overhead front toss (Figure A), side toss (Figure B), or scoop toss (Figure C).

Figure A. Overhead front toss

Figure B. Side toss

Figure C. Scoop toss

#52: Medicine Ball Tennis

Skills Developed: Aerobic/anaerobic conditioning, agility, muscular strength/endurance, and power

Players: 2–4

Playing Area: Tennis court

Materials Needed: Large medicine ball (weight determined by the size and strength of the athletes)

Description: Begin by pairing athletes of similar size and strength. The rules of tennis apply to this game. However, rather than using a racket and tennis ball, this game is played using a medicine ball. The object is to throw the medicine ball over the net using the motions used in tennis: overhand (Figure A), backhand (Figure B), and forehand (Figure C). These actions should require the athletes to rotate their bodies to throw the medicine ball over the net. The receiving athlete must catch the ball before it bounces twice. If the medicine ball does bounce twice before it is caught, a point is scored by the serving athlete. If the medicine ball does not bounce twice, play continues. To be effective, athletes should throw the medicine ball using as few steps as possible (i.e., without wasting time), thus giving the opposing athlete as little time as possible to recover from his last serve. The game is over when an athlete wins the best of three sets. A set is won when an athlete scores six points. However, the set must be won by at least two points.

Notes:

• If using a tennis court, the athletes should use the appropriate lines accordingly (i.e., singles or doubles). If a tennis court is not used, the boundaries of the utilized playing area can be marked with cones or chalk.

Variations:

• Use a reaction ball.

• The athletes can play for time rather than sets.

Figure A. Overhead throw

Figure B. Backhand throw

Figure C. Forehand throw

#53: Monkey See, Monkey Do

Skills Developed: Aerobic/anaerobic conditioning, agility, balance, coordination, muscular strength/endurance, reaction, and recovery

Players: 2–5

Playing Area: Open area

Materials Needed: None

Description: Begin by designating one athlete to be the leader. Instruct the leader to stand facing the other athletes. The leader's job is to perform physical movements (everything from standing on a single leg to performing short sprints), which the other athletes must mimic. For example, if the leader runs forward and immediately switches to a lateral carioca, the other athletes should do the same. The athletes repeat this process for a predetermined amount of time or until the mimicking athletes have fallen significantly behind.

Variations:

- Instruct the athletes to perform the opposite of what the leader performs (reversed mimicking).

- Limit the movements performed by the leader (e.g., only lateral movement).

- Add various pieces of equipment, such as agility ladders, medicine balls, or cones.

#54: Musketeers

Skills Developed: Aerobic conditioning, agility, reaction, teamwork, and timing

Players: 6 or more

Playing Area: Large open area

Materials Needed: Cones/markers to outline boundaries

Description: Divide the athletes into groups of three or four. Then, instruct each group to distinguish one athlete as the king. Also, designate one athlete, who is unassigned to a group, as the assassin. At the whistle, the assassin attempts to tag the king. Each group works together to keep the assassin from tagging its kings (see figure). If the king is tagged, the assassin then gets to choose an athlete to replace him as the assassin, and the former assassin becomes the new king for that group. The athletes play for a designated amount of time.

Variations:

• Attach resistance tubing to the athletes' legs or hips.

• Add incentives (e.g., if a group's royalty is tagged, then the group must perform 10 push-ups before the game can resume).

Players defending the royalty from the chaser

#55: Noodle Gladiators

Skills Developed: Balance and stability

Players: 2

Playing Area: Open area

Materials Needed: 2 swim noodles and 2 balance discs/wobble boards

Description: Athletes begin by facing each other while standing on balance discs or wobble boards that are positioned approximately three to four feet apart from each other. At the whistle, the athletes use the swim noodles to knock their opponents off balance. Only strikes below an athlete's neck are allowed. The athlete who wins two out of three matches is declared the victor.

Variation:

- The athletes can perform this game on a balance beam or other balance device.

#56: Out

Skills Developed: Aerobic/anaerobic conditioning, agility, balance, coordination, muscular strength/endurance, and reaction

Players: 6 or more

Playing Area: Open area

Materials Needed: Medicine ball (weight based on the strength of the athletes)

Description: This game is similar to Hot Ball (#33) in the formation of the playing area and the passing of the ball. However, the medicine ball is not passed for an allotted amount of time, but until an athlete drops it. When an athlete drops the medicine ball, or throws a bad pass, he receives a letter (i.e., "O"). Any athlete who spells the word "out" is eliminated and must run laps until the next athlete is out. Once that occurs, the runner then performs push-ups and sit-ups while the most recently eliminated athlete runs laps. This cycle repeats until only one athlete remains.

Variations:

- Require the athletes to perform 10 push-ups after they drop the medicine ball.

- Use two medicine balls in the circle.

- Use longer or shorter words instead of "out" (e.g., the team's mascot, such as Eagles or Panthers).

#57: Pace Master

Skills Developed: Aerobic conditioning and cognitive awareness

Players: 2 or more

Playing Area: Quarter-mile track

Materials Needed: Stopwatch, paper, and pencil

Description: After a proper warm-up, pair athletes of similar ability and designate one athlete to run the quarter-mile as quickly as possible. The other athlete manages the stopwatch. The athletes repeat this process so that everyone completes the run. Next, bring the groups together and explain the concept of pacing and the necessity for pacing during competition. Then, have the athletes come up with one or two strategies that they can use to pace themselves. For example, if an athlete runs the lap in 60 seconds, instruct him to run the lap 10 to 30 seconds slower. The goal is to find a pace that is fast enough to develop cardiovascular endurance. Instruct the athletes to practice pacing until a steady pace can be maintained.

Variation:

• Set up cones or flags to mark every 100 yards to help the pacing process.

#58: Pass Interference

Skills Developed: Aerobic/anaerobic conditioning, agility, balance, coordination, reaction, and teamwork

Players: 8 or more

Playing Area: Large open area (preferably a football field)

Materials Needed: 1 ball, 2 sets of jerseys, and cones (optional)

Description: Divide the athletes into two teams. One team begins with the ball in the end zone. Much like "ultimate Frisbee®," the object of the game is to move the ball down to the other end zone as quickly as possible without losing control of the ball. However, the athlete in control of the ball is unable to run. Instead, he is only allowed to pivot. The defending team's goal is to stop the other team from scoring using a one-on-one defensive strategy. However, they must do so by staying at least one-and-a-half arm-lengths from the offensive athlete. If a team scores, the ball is dropped in the end zone, and the defending team then becomes the offensive team. The ball can be turned over if it is intercepted or goes out of bounds. The team with the most points at the end of a certain amount of time wins.

Variations:

• The athletes can play continuously until a team accumulates five or more points.

• Allow the athlete in control of the ball to take one, two, or three steps.

• Allow the defending team to play a zone defense.

• Use different objects as the ball (e.g., medicine balls, Frisbees).

#59: Pass Precision

Skills Developed: Aerobic conditioning, agility, reaction, and teamwork

Players: 6 or more

Playing Area: Large field

Materials Needed: 2 soccer balls (different colors or styles), jerseys, and a stop watch

Description: Divide the athletes equally into two teams. One team controls the ball and the other team attempts to stop or steal the ball. The object of the game is similar to "keep away." However, points are only scored by striking one ball against the other. At the whistle, the five-minute clock begins and the ball is put into play. The team in control of the ball attempts to move the ball around the field without it being stolen by the opposing team. At your discretion, the second ball is thrown into play. Then, the goal is for the team in control of the ball to strike the other ball with the one already in play (see figure). The athletes, however, must stay at least six feet from the second ball. Once the ball is hit, a point is scored, at which point you retrieve the ball from the field to throw out at a later time. The team with the most points wins.

Variations:

- The athletes can use different types of balls (e.g., football, medicine ball, tennis ball).

- Leave the scoring object on the field the entire time.

- Allow the athletes to play for a predetermined set of points (rather than time).

Athlete attempting to score a point by striking the second ball

#60: Pay it Forward

Skills Developed: Aerobic/anaerobic conditioning, muscular strength/endurance, and teamwork

Players: 8 or more

Playing Area: Large open area (approximately 50 yards long)

Materials Needed: Heavy objects (e.g., medicine balls, sandbags, water jugs) and 8 cones/markers

Description: Divide the athletes equally into teams. One cone is designated as the starting line, from which cones are positioned 15 yards, 25 yards, and 40 yards away (see figure). Have one athlete stand at the 15-yard cone and another stand at the 25-yard cone. The other athletes remain behind the starting line, each holding a heavy object that they are not allowed to set down. At the whistle, the first athlete in line sprints to the 15-yard cone and hands off his object to the athlete standing there, replacing it with another heavy object. After receiving the object, the athlete at the cone will sprint to the 25-yard marker and hand off his heavy object to the athlete standing there. Lastly, this athlete sprints to the 40-yard cone. Once he reaches the final cone, the next athlete in line can begin. This process continues until all of the athletes have switched sides, at which point they repeat the process back to the starting line. The team whose athletes make it down and back first wins.

Variations:

• Position the cones closer or further apart (depending on the training effect desired).

• Require athletes to perform an activity when they reach each cone (e.g., push-ups, squats, sit-ups).

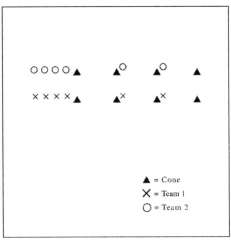

Set-up and player formation for Pay it Forward

#61: Pepper

Skills Developed: Coordination and reaction

Players: 3–5

Playing Area: Open area

Materials Needed: 1 home plate marker, 1 foam/Wiffle ball bat, and 1 foam/Wiffle ball

Description: This game is commonly used by baseball and softball athletes as a warm-up. Designate one athlete as the batter and instruct the remainder of the athletes (i.e., the fielders) to line up approximately 10 to 15 feet away. The fielders then toss the ball to the batter, who attempts to hit it back to them. The batter is retired when he fails to hit a ball tossed in the strike zone (i.e., over the plate and between the lower portion of the chest and knees), or if one of the field athletes catches a hit ball in the air. The object of the game is to become the batter and hit as many tossed balls on the ground before being retired. A fielder who catches the ball becomes the new batter, all other field athletes rotate to the left, and the previous batter assumes the end fielding position (i.e., the farthest position to the right).

#62: Possession

Skills Developed: Aerobic/anaerobic conditioning, agility, manipulative skills, and reaction

Players: 4 or more

Playing Area: Large open area (preferably a gymnasium)

Materials Needed: 2 stopwatches, 1 ball (e.g., volleyball, basketball, medicine ball), or a Frisbee

Description: Divide the athletes equally into two teams. Both teams randomly spread out across the playing area. Then, one athlete is selected from each team to go to the center of the playing area. The timekeeper throws the ball into the air, at which time the athletes perform a jump ball to begin the game. As soon as an athlete takes possession of the ball, the timekeeper gives the signal and the stopwatch is started for that athlete's team. Athletes may either run with the ball or pass it to a teammate while being pursued by the opposing team's athletes. When the athlete holding the ball is tagged, the timekeeper stops the stopwatch, and the athlete holding the ball must immediately stop running and toss the ball to the closest member of the opposing team. As soon as the ball is received, the timekeeper again gives the signal and the stopwatch is started for the team with possession of the ball. At the end of the game, the team that kept possession of the ball for the longest period of time is the winner.

Note:

- The timekeeper must keep two stopwatches (one for each team).

#63: Power Ball

Skills Developed: Aerobic/anaerobic conditioning, agility, manipulative skills, and speed

Players: 4 or more

Playing Area: Large open area (preferably a football field or gymnasium)

Materials Needed: 2 large trash cans, 8 cones, and 1 basketball or football

Description: This game is a combination of American football, basketball, and tag. A large trash can is positioned at approximately the same place on both sides of the playing area, with a square safety area measuring approximately 10 feet by 10 feet surrounding each can (Figure A). After dividing the athletes equally into two teams, instruct each team to go to its side of the playing area. One team begins the game as the offense and the other as the defense. The game starts when a designated athlete on the defensive team puts the ball into play by throwing it to the offensive team's side of the playing field. When an athlete catches the ball, he is allowed to run toward the opponent's trash can (goal) until he is tagged. The athletes are allowed to pass the ball to other teammates before being tagged. Once tagged, the athlete with possession of the ball must stop in place, drop the ball, and allow the opposing team to gain possession of the ball. A point is scored each time an athlete successfully shoots the ball into the other team's trash can without entering the safety area surrounding it (Figure B). Each team receives one point for each goal scored from outside the square. If an athlete enters the square, his team loses possession of the ball. If the athlete scores a goal while in the square, one point is added to the opposing team's final score. If a throw is intercepted, or a point is scored, the defensive team then becomes the offensive team

Variation:

*   Restrict the athletes to tossing the ball underhand when shooting a goal.

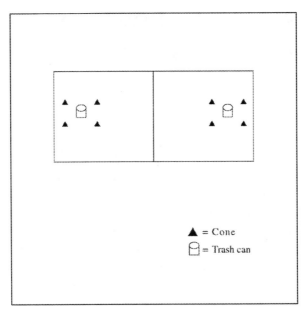

Figure A. Set-up for Power Ball

Figure B. Athlete attempting to score a goal

#64: Pull for Time Tug-of-War

Skills Developed: Muscular strength/endurance, stability, reaction, and speed

Players: 2 or more

Playing Area: Open area

Materials Needed: 1 long rope, 1 flag/marker, 1 stopwatch, and 1 cone

Description: Divide the athletes equally into two teams and have them hold the rope in preparation for a tug-of-war. Securely fasten a flag or marker at the center of the rope and position the flag over a cone between the two teams. After both teams are lined up properly on the rope awaiting the whistle, announce that the pull is to be conducted for a specific amount of time (e.g., 30 seconds, one minute). The team with the flag on its side of the cone when time runs out wins the match.

#65: Pull for the Cone Tug-of-War

Skills Developed: Muscular strength/endurance, stability, reaction, and speed

Players: 2 or more

Playing Area: Open area

Materials Needed: 1 large rope, 2 cones, and 2 tennis balls or racquetballs

Description: This game is played like traditional tug-of-war, with only a few differences. After stretching the length of the rope on the ground, position a cone with a tennis ball placed on top four to five feet away from each end of the rope. The last athlete on each team holds on with one hand while turning to face the cone. At the whistle, both teams try to pull hard enough to allow their end person (i.e., the anchor) to either grab or knock the ball off the top of the cone with his hands or feet (see figure). The first team to accomplish this task is declared the winner.

Athlete attempting to knock the ball off the cone

#66: Rectangle Madness

Skills Developed: Anaerobic conditioning, agility, balance, coordination, reaction, and teamwork

Players: 12 or more

Playing Area: Large open area

Materials Needed: Jerseys (optional) and 4–8 soft foam/rubber balls

Description: Divide the playing area into four adjacent rectangles and divide the athletes equally into two teams. Each of the teams should divide into two parts and stand in alternate rectangles of the playing area, as shown in the figure. Position two or three balls on each of the lines between the zones. At the whistle, the athletes collect the balls as quickly as possible and begin throwing them at the opposing team. If an athlete is hit, he must run to the sidelines, perform 30 speed squats, and then rejoin his team. When an athlete hits another athlete with a ball or catches a ball, his team receives one point. If the ball is caught, then the athlete who threw the ball must go to the sidelines and perform 10 squat thrusts before rejoining his team and the game. At the end of designated time (e.g., five minutes), the team with the most points wins.

Variations:

- Use the same playing area layout, but with four separate teams.

- Use more or fewer balls to challenge the athletes.

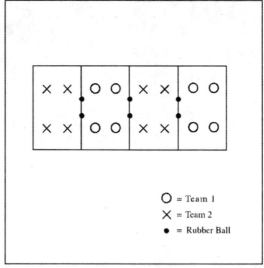

Set-up and Player formation for Rectangle Madness

#67: Relay Golf

Skills Developed: Aerobic conditioning, muscular strength/power, speed, and teamwork

Players: 2 or more

Playing Area: Large open area

Materials Needed: 9 hula hoops, 9 cones, 1 object per pair of players (e.g., football, Frisbee, medicine ball), pencil, and paper

Description: Begin by setting up a golf course using the cones as the tee box and hula hoops as the holes. The object of the game is similar to golf. However, rather than hitting the ball, the athletes pass the ball to each other. One athlete begins at the tee box, and the other athlete runs down the fairway to the hula hoop, or hole, to catch the ball. If the ball is caught, then the athlete who threw the ball becomes the receiving athlete. He then runs down past the first receiving athlete (now the thrower) to the next hula hoop and attempts to catch the ball. If the ball is dropped, the team is penalized one stroke, and the throw must be attempted again. Record the number of throws attempted for each hole. The team with the least throws wins.

Variations:

- Assign a par based on the distance and difficulty of the holes (e.g., a 50-yard hole may have a par of five to 15, depending on the object being thrown).

- Designate hand usage for particular holes (e.g., hole 2, par eight, left-hand throwing only).

- Prohibit the receiving athlete from standing on two feet, instead requiring him to hop on one foot while playing (switching feet with every hole).

#68: Rip City

Skills Developed: Agility and speed

Players: 2 or more

Playing Area: Large open area

Materials Needed: Flags (the quantity depends on the number of athletes)

Description: This game is played just like tag, except everyone is "it." Each athlete has one flag tucked into the waistband of his shorts or pants on the right or left hip, with the majority of the flag showing. Athletes then randomly spread out over the playing area and await the whistle. The object of the game is for each athlete to grab an opposing athlete's flag without having his own flag taken in the process. If an athlete's flag is taken, then that athlete must perform various conditioning exercises or jog around the playing area until the end of the game. The last athlete still possessing his flag wins.

#69: Rock Wrestle

Skills Developed: Muscular strength/endurance, reaction, power, and stability

Players: 2

Playing Area: Open area

Materials Needed: None

Description: Two athletes stand back to back while linking arms at the elbows. At the whistle, both athletes attempt to lean forward and lift their opponent into the air and onto their back. The athlete who wins two out of three matches is declared the winner.

Note:

• The athletes should be approximately the same size and possess roughly the same amount of strength.

#70: Rooster Fight

Skills Developed: Balance, muscular strength/endurance, power, and stability

Players: 2

Playing Area: Open area

Materials Needed: 2 pairs of football shoulder pads

Description: Two athletes stand face to face approximately three feet apart. They each grab the inside of their ankles with the palms facing out and the thumbs back (see figure). At the whistle, both athletes ram each other using only their shoulder pads to force their opponent off balance or make him let go of his ankles. The athlete who wins two out of three matches is declared the winner.

Note:

- The athletes should be approximately the same size and possess roughly the same amount of strength.

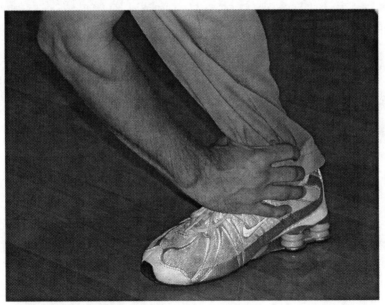

Hand position for Rooster Fight

#71: Scramble Tug-of-War

Skills Developed: Muscular strength/endurance, power, reaction, speed, and stability

Players: 2 or more

Playing Area: Large open area

Materials Needed: 1 large rope

Description: After stretching the length of the rope on the ground, instruct the athletes to assume a push-up position (or lie on their backs with their feet touching the rope) (see figure). At the whistle, the athletes jump up, grab the rope, and begin pulling. The rules governing each tug-of-war may vary.

Variation:

• Set up the match as a pull for distance, pull for time, or pull for the cone (refer to #64 and #65).

Set-up for Scramble Tug-of-War with the athletes on their backs

#72: Sharks and Minnows

Skills Developed: Aerobic/anaerobic conditioning, agility, balance, coordination, muscular strength/endurance, and reaction

Players: 10 or more

Playing Area: Large open area

Materials Needed: 4 cones and flags (e.g., old rags/cloth strips, flag football belts; the number of flags needed is dependent upon the number of players)

Description: Use the cones to create a playing area measuring 40 yards by 20 yards (see figure). Select two athletes to be the sharks. Distribute flags to the other athletes, who are the minnows. The sharks are stationed in the playing area, and the minnows are on either end of the playing area. At the whistle, the minnows attempt to sprint from end to end without allowing the sharks to get their flags. When a minnow is caught, he must run laps until the game is over. The game continues until two minnows remain. The last two minnows become the new sharks for the next game.

Note:

- The flags can be lightly stuffed into the pockets of the minnows or placed in the elastic of their shorts/pants.

Variation:

- Adjust the size of the playing area (making it smaller or larger depending on conditioning goals and/or team size).

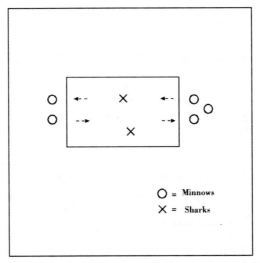

Set-up and player formation for Sharks and Minnows

#73: Shoulder Wrestle

Skills Developed: Balance, muscular strength/endurance, power, and stability

Players: 2 athletes of equal size and ability

Area: Open area

Materials Needed: A 10-feet by 10-feet mat or 4 cones/markers

Description: The athletes begin by getting on all-fours while facing each other. At the whistle, each athlete tries to drive his opponent off the mat or out of the designated area marked by the cones/markers using only his right shoulder (see figure). The athletes should alternate right and left shoulders, or use both, from match to match. The athlete who wins two out of three matches is declared the winner.

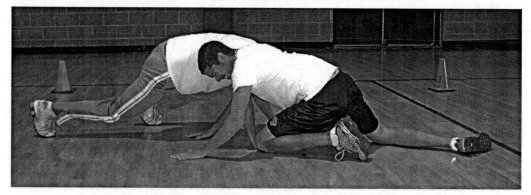

Athletes attempting to drive their opponent out of the playing area

#74: Single-Leg Tug-of-War

Skills Developed: Balance, muscular strength/endurance, power, and stability

Players: 2

Playing Area: Large open area

Materials Needed: 1 rope or resistance chord

Description: Instruct the athletes to assume a single-leg stance on either side of the rope. Both athletes then pick up the rope, gently pull it to remove any slack, and wait for the whistle. At the whistle, the athletes simply pull. The athlete who can maintain his balance for the longest time wins. Instruct the athletes to perform this game on both the right and left legs.

#75: Sled Race

Skills Developed: Aerobic/anaerobic conditioning and muscular strength/endurance

Players: 6 or more

Playing Area: Large open grass field (or artificial turf)

Materials Needed: 1 sled and 1 rope

Description: Divide the athletes into teams and then pair each individual athlete with another athlete from his own team of equal size and/or strength. Instruct one athlete to sit on the sled and have his partner grab the rope tied to the sled. Thus, one athlete serves as the rider and one athlete serves as the puller. At the whistle, the pulling athlete pulls the sled for 10 yards. Once the sled passes the 10-yard mark, the athletes switch places and the new pulling athlete pulls the sled and its rider back to the starting line. When they complete the task, the next pair of athletes takes its turn until all of the pairs of athletes have served as riders and pullers. The first team to cross the finish line wins.

Variation:

• Tie a longer rope to the sled and instruct each team of athletes to pull one of its teammates as fast as possible.

#76: Smacks

Skill Developed: Reaction

Players: 2

Playing Area: Open area

Materials Needed: 2 focus mitts (frequently used in martial arts)

Description: Two athletes stand face to face approximately three feet apart. Instruct one of those athletes to place a focus mitt on each hand so that the back of his hands are covered. Next, the two athletes extend their arms out at chest level, pressing the palms together in a prayer-like position. At the whistle, the athlete not wearing the mitts, the smacker, attempts to slap the hands of the athlete wearing mitts as many times as possible in one minute. The athlete wearing mitts attempts to avoid being smacked by moving his hands up and down. After one minute, the athletes switch roles. The athlete that has the greatest number of smacks after one minute is declared the winner.

#77: Soccer Dodgeball

Skills Developed: Agility, coordination, reaction, and speed

Players: 10–15

Materials Needed: 1 slightly deflated playground ball or beach ball and 1 stopwatch

Playing Area: Large open area

Description: This game is set up and played in a similar manner as Circle Dodgeball (#9). The athletes form a circle and one athlete stands in the middle of that circle. At the whistle, start the stopwatch as the athletes forming the circle kick the deflated playground ball in an attempt to hit the center athlete (aiming below the neck). Once the center athlete is hit, he rotates to the circle, and the next athlete in line, as designated by you, rotates to the center. This game is continued until each athlete has gone at least once. The athlete who stays in the center for the longest time before being hit by the ball wins.

Note:

- A 10-second penalty should be given to any circle athlete who hits a center athlete above the waist.

#78: Sprint Tug-of-War

Skills Developed: Power, muscular strength/endurance, stability, reaction, and speed

Players: 2 or more

Playing Area: Large open area

Materials Needed: 1 large rope and cones/markers

Description: This game can be set up as a pull for distance, pull for time, or pull for the cone. After dividing the athletes into two teams and stretching the length of the rope on the ground, measure approximately 10 to 15 feet away from the rope on each end and set up a cone/marker where the teams will line up. At the whistle, the athletes sprint, grab the rope, and begin pulling. The winner of the match is dictated by the rules of the specific tug-of-war game selected.

#79: Squat War

Skills Developed: Balance, muscular strength/endurance, power, and stability

Players: 2 athletes of equal size and ability

Playing Area: Open area free of sharp objects and clutter

Materials Needed: 4 balance discs or devices and 1 medicine ball

Description: While standing approximately five feet apart and facing one another, the athletes place each foot on a balance disc and assume a squat position (this position should be held for the duration of the match). At the whistle, one athlete picks up the medicine ball and passes it to his opponent in an attempt to force him off balance. The game continues until a player is unable to maintain his balance or can no longer maintain the squat position.

Variation:

• Allow only one type of toss to be performed (e.g., chest pass, underhand toss).

#80: Stool Burner Race

Skill Developed: Strength

Players: 2 or more

Playing Area: Large open area (preferably a gymnasium)

Materials Needed: Square stools with wheels or scooters (the quanity depends on the number of athletes) and cones (optional)

Description: Instruct the athletes to line up at one end of the playing area on the starting line or behind a cone. Once there, each athlete sits on a stool/scooter while grasping the sides of the seat (Figure A). At the whistle, the athletes "walk" the stool/scooter forward. The first athlete to cross the finish line (or cone) at the other end of the playing area is the winner (Figure B).

Note:

- Racers should not contact any other racer or scooter during this race.

Variations:

- Increase the distance traveled.

- Create relays.

- Require players to extend their arms and hold them up as they travel forward.

Figure A. Athlete performing a stool burner

Figure B. Athletes racing

#81: Stubborn Mule

Skills Developed: Balance, muscular strength/endurance, power, and stability

Players: 2 athletes of equal size and ability

Playing Area: Large open area

Materials Needed: Stopwatch

Description: Divide the athletes into pairs, with one athlete designated as the mule and the other athlete as the carrier. The mule places his hands on the floor and extends his legs up. The carrier then grabs the mule by the ankles and holds them close to his own hips (see figure). At the whistle, the mule attempts to pull the carrier off balance by rapidly moving forward on his hands. The carrier resists the mule and attempts to maintain his balance as the mule forcefully drives forward. If the carrier has been pulled off balance or the mule gives up, the athletes switch positions. The athlete able to maintain his balance for the longest time is the winner.

Variation:

• Establish a predetermined mark five to 10 feet in front of the mule across which the mule should attempt to pull the carrier.

Stubborn Mule position

#82: Submerge and Retrieve

Skills Developed: Aerobic/anaerobic conditioning and muscular strength/endurance

Players: 6 or more

Playing Area: Swimming pool

Materials Needed: Sinkable, preferably color-coded, objects (the quantity is equal to the number of participants) and 2 buckets/containers

Description: Begin by throwing all the sinkable objects into the deep end of a swimming pool. Divide the athletes who can swim into teams and instruct them to line up at the shallow end of the swimming pool. At the whistle, the first athlete in line sits on the edge of the swimming pool and slowly slides into the water. He then swims to the bottom of the deep end and retrieves an object. He then swims back to the starting line and places his object in the bucket, which signals the next athlete to enter the pool. This process continues until all of the objects have been retrieved. The first team to collect all of its objects wins.

Notes:

- A lifeguard is required for this activity.

- Players that are unable to swim should be given an alternative activity.

Variations:

- Place 10 objects on the bottom of the pool. The team to retrieve the most objects in a predetermined amount of time wins.

- Use coins or smaller objects.

- Use heavier objects (e.g., medicine balls, sand bags, dumbbells).

#83: Sumo Wrestling

Skills Developed: Aerobic/anaerobic conditioning, agility, muscular strength/endurance, and power

Players: 2 or more

Playing Area: A ring measuring 15 feet by 15 feet

Materials Needed: 2 blocker shields and 2 helmets (optional)

Description: The rules of this game are similar to sumo wrestling. However, rather than the athletes pushing each other with their hands, they use blockers in attempt to push one another out of the ring (see figure). The use of the blocker helps equalize the athletes and incorporates more strategy, rather than allowing the athletes to rely solely on brute strength. The athlete who successfully wins two out of three matches moves on to the next round of matches. The game ends when only one athlete remains.

Variations:

- Use a smaller ring.

- Instruct the athletes to begin at starting lines two feet from each other.

- Use smaller or larger blockers.

Athletes attempting to drive each other out of the playing area

#84: Swimming Through Hoops

Skills Developed: Aerobic/anaerobic conditioning, agility, coordination, and muscular strength/endurance

Players: 6 or more

Playing Area: Swimming pool

Materials Needed: 6 hula hoops, multiple strands of rope or strong tape, and 6 bricks

Description: Begin by attaching a brick to each of the hula hoops using rope or tape and carefully placing them into the swimming pool, spaced equally into two rows. Divide the athletes equally into two teams and instruct them to stand at the edge of the shallow end of the swimming pool. At the whistle, the first athlete in line jumps into the water and swims through all three hoops, coming up for air as often as needed. Once the athlete swims through the third hoop, he must touch the wall and swim back to tag the next athlete in line. This process is repeated until the last athlete has touched the starting wall. The first team to successfully swim through all the hoops is the winner.

Note:

- A lifeguard is required for this activity.

Variations:

- Position the hula hoops in a zigzag pattern under water.

- Instruct the athletes to collect objects while swimming through the hoops (e.g., each athlete must return with three coins).

#85: Swiss Ball War

Skills Developed: Balance, power, and stability

Players: 2 or more

Playing Area: Open area

Materials Needed: 1 Swiss ball for each athlete

Description: Holding a Swiss ball against their chests, the athletes hop on one leg and attempt to push the opposing athletes off balance (see figure). In the process, the athletes should not hit or make direct physical contact with an opposing athlete with anything other than the Swiss ball, which should remain against the chest at all times. Any other contact results in an automatic disqualification. In addition, if an athlete touches the floor with his free foot, he is disqualified and must perform a predetermined skill (e.g., push-ups, squats) on the sideline until a winner is declared.

Variation:

• The athletes can alternate legs.

Athletes attempting to knock each other off balance by hitting the Swiss balls

#86: Swiss Ball Wrestle

Skills Developed: Balance, muscular strength/endurance, and stability

Players: 2 athletes of equal size and ability

Playing Area: Open area free of sharp object s and clutter

Materials Needed: 1 large Swiss ball

Description: Two athletes assume a good athletic position (i.e., chest up, shoulders back, and knees, hips, and feet approximately shoulder-width apart) while holding the Swiss ball (see figure). At the whistle, each athlete tries to wrestle the ball away from the other while protecting his own Swiss ball.

Variations:

- Substitute in a medicine ball.

- The athletes can perform this game on one leg.

- The athletes can perform this game in a kneeling position (with both athletes' knees on a wrestling/exercise mat).

Athlete attempting to wrestle the Swiss ball away from her opponent

#87: Team Keep Away

Skills Developed: Aerobic/anaerobic conditioning, agility, reaction, and speed

Players: 6 or more

Playing Area: Large open area

Materials Needed: 1 ball (e.g., basketball, volleyball, football) and 1 stopwatch

Description: After dividing the athletes equally into two teams, instruct them to spread out in their designated playing areas. At the whistle, start the stopwatch and pass the ball to one of the teams. The team in possession of the ball passes it among themselves while trying to prevent the other team from gaining possession. Athletes may pass, intercept, and strip the ball as necessary to gain possession of it. This game is best played for a predetermined amount of time. The team in possession of the ball at the end of the predetermined time wins.

#88: Teammate Carry

Skill Developed: Muscular strength/endurance

Players: 6 or more

Playing Area: Large open area

Materials Needed: 2 cones/markers

Description: Divide athletes of equal size and strength into groups of three. Two of the athletes in each group face each other, grasp their own left wrists with their right hands, and then use their left hand to grasp their teammate's right wrist while their teammate does the same to them (Figure A). The third athlete on the team sits on the seat created by his two teammates while holding on to his teammates' shoulders to remain balanced (Figure B). The object of the game is for each team of athletes to carry its teammate for a predetermined distance and then back again to the starting point. Upon returning to the starting point, the athletes switch positions. This process is repeated until each athlete has been carried across the starting marker. If the athlete being carried is dropped or touches the ground during the relay, then his team must go back to the last marker passed and repeat this process. The team to complete this task in the least amount of time wins the relay.

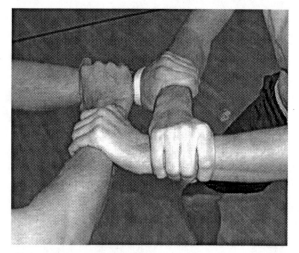

Figure A. Forming the seat

Figure B. An athlete being carried

#89: T-Shirt Shuffle

Skills Developed: Aerobic conditioning, muscular endurance, and teamwork

Players: 4 or more

Playing Area: Swimming pool

Materials Needed: Large T-shirts (the quantity is equal to the number of teams; shirts must fit the largest athlete)

Description: Divide the athletes into teams, with the number and size of the teams depending on the number of athletes as well as the size of the swimming pool. Each team then splits up evenly, with each half going to opposite sides of the pool. At the whistle, the first athlete puts on the T-shirt, jumps into the swimming pool, and swims across. The athlete then takes off the T-shirt and hands it to the next athlete. The next athlete must have the shirt completely on (i.e., arms and head through the proper holes) before jumping into the swimming pool. This process continues until all of the athletes have crossed the pool. The first team to have all of its athletes switch sides wins.

Note:

- A lifeguard is required for this activity

Variations:

- Instruct the athletes to swim the length of the pool twice before giving the T-shirt to the next in line.

- Require the athletes to wear old shoes while swimming.

- Designate a particular stroke to be used while swimming (e.g., breast stroke, side stroke, doggy paddle).

- Instruct the athletes to run (in the water) rather than swim.

#90: Tug Wrestle

Skills Developed: Balance, muscular strength/endurance, power, and stability

Players: 2 athletes of equal size and ability

Playing Area: Open area free of clutter and sharp objects

Materials Needed: 1 marker

Description: Two athletes begin by facing each other while grabbing their opponent's right wrist. At the whistle, each athlete attempts to pull his opponent across a predetermined line/marker on the floor between the athletes (see figure). The athletes then switch to the left wrist and repeat.

Variations:

• Alternate the way the game is played (e.g., two-handed tug wrestle in which the athletes hold both wrists).

• Instruct the athletes to perform this game on one leg, switching legs with each match.

Athlete attempting to pull his opponent over the center line

#91: Twister

Skills Developed: Anaerobic conditioning, balance, coordination, muscular strength/endurance, and reaction

Players: 12 or more

Playing Area: Large open area

Materials Needed: 2 medicine balls

Description: Divide the athletes equally into two teams and instruct the athletes on each team to line up in a straight line with 10 to 12 feet between each athlete. The first athlete in each line holds the medicine ball. At the whistle, the first athlete in line throws the ball to the next athlete by rotating to his left (see figure). After throwing the medicine ball, the first athlete in line faces the front again while the second athlete throws the ball to the third athlete in line. This process continues down the line as quickly as possible. Once the ball reaches the end of the line, the athletes turn around and repeat the process by throwing the ball over their right shoulders. The first team to get the medicine ball down and back wins.

Variations:

*   Require the athletes to throw the ball over their heads.

*   Instruct the athletes to throw the ball in between their feet.

*   Use a water-filled ball or other unstable ball.

*   Adjust the distance between the athletes.

An athlete passing the medicine ball to his teammate

#92: Ultimate

Skills Developed: Agility, manipulative skills, reaction, and speed

Players: 8 or more

Playing Area: Football field

Materials Needed: 1 Frisbee and multiple cones/markers (optional)

Description: The rules to this game are similar to football. However, limited physical contact is allowed and the receiving athlete's role is slightly modified. After dividing the athletes equally into two teams, instruct each team to go to its side of the playing area. One team begins the game as the offense and the other team begins as the defense. The game starts when a designated athlete on the defensive team puts the Frisbee in play by throwing it to the offensive team's side of the playing field. When an athlete on the offensive team catches or picks up the Frisbee, that athlete must remain stationary and throw the Frisbee to an athlete on his team. This process is repeated to move the Frisbee down the playing area toward the opponent's goal line. A point is scored each time an athlete crosses his opponent's goal line and catches the Frisbee in the air. If a throw is intercepted, or if a point is scored, then the defensive team becomes the offensive team.

Variation:

•   Use a ball instead of a Frisbee.

#93: Ultimate Tag

Skills Developed: Agility, manipulative skills, reaction, and speed

Players: 8 or more

Playing Area: Large open area

Materials Needed: 1 Frisbee and multiple cones/markers (optional)

Description: The rules of this game are the same as Ultimate (#92), with a few exceptions. When a receiving athlete catches the Frisbee, he is allowed to run toward the opponent's goal until he is tagged. Once tagged, he must stop in place, release the Frisbee, and the other team immediately gains possession.

Variation:

•   Use a ball instead of a Frisbee.

#94: Ultimate Square Off

Skills Developed: Anaerobic conditioning, agility, balance, coordination, reaction, and teamwork

Players: 12 or more

Playing Area: Large open area (divided into 4 equal areas)

Materials Needed: Jerseys (optional) and 4–8 soft foam or rubber balls

Description: Divide the playing area using a large four-square design (see figure) and divide the athletes equally into two teams. Each team should divide itself in half and stand in alternate squares of the playing area, as shown in the figure. Place four to eight balls in the center of the four squares and instruct the athletes to line up on the side opposite the balls. At the whistle, the athletes sprint to gather the balls and begin throwing them at each other. If an athlete is hit, he must run to the side of the playing area, perform 10 squat thrusts, and then return to his team on the playing area. The athlete who hits another athlete with a ball, or catches a ball, earns one point for his team. If a ball is caught, the thrower must run to the side of the playing area and perform 30 speed squats before returning to the game. At the end of the designated amount of time, the team with the most points wins.

Variations:

- Use the same four-square layout, but with four separate teams. The team with the most points at the end wins.

- Use more or fewer balls to challenge the athletes.

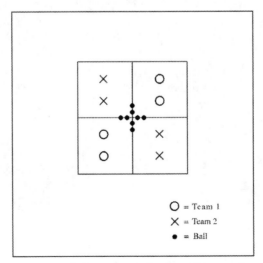

Set-up and player formation for Ultimate Square Off

#95: Upper-Body Blitz

Skills Developed: Muscular strength/endurance, and power

Players: 2 or more

Playing Area: Large open area (preferably a gymnasium)

Materials Needed: Scooters and multiple cones/markers (optional)

Description: The athletes position themselves on the starting line, kneel onto the scooters, and place their hands on the ground directly to the sides and just in front of the scooters (see figure). At the whistle, the athletes use their arms, back, and shoulders to forcefully pull themselves forward. The athlete who crosses the finish line (cone/marker) at the other end of the playing area in the shortest amount of time is the winner.

Note:

• Athletes may not contact any other athlete or their scooters during this race.

Variations:

• Increase the distance traveled by the athletes.

• The athletes can perform relays.

An athlete kneeling on a scooter

#96: Wall Ball

Skills Developed: Agility, coordination, manipulative skills, and speed

Players: 2

Playing Area: Open area with a smooth-surface wall (preferably a racquetball court).

Materials Needed: Racquetball

Description: The game begins with the serving athlete throwing the racquetball and bouncing it off the wall. The second athlete is allowed one bounce before he must catch the ball and throw it against the wall (see figure). Throws are alternated until an athlete allows the ball to bounce more than once before he can catch it. A point is awarded to an athlete each time his opponent fails to successfully catch the ball before the second bounce or when a throw is missed.

Variation:

• Instruct the athletes to catch and throw the ball using only the nondominant arm.

An athlete throwing the ball

#97: Water Polo

Skills Developed: Aerobic/anaerobic conditioning, agility, coordination, muscular strength/endurance, and reaction

Players: 6 or more

Playing Area: Swimming pool

Materials Needed: Small rubber ball or slightly deflated volleyball, hockey nets or cones

Description: This game can be played either in the shallow or deep end of a swimming pool. The depth of the pool is determined by the swimming abilities of the athletes. Mark goals with cones on each side of the swimming pool and place one cone on the side of the playing area to designate the center. Divide the athletes equally into two teams and instruct the athletes to move into the playing area. If you are working with more than 10 total athletes, the remaining athletes should stand on the outside of the swimming pool to retrieve balls thrown out of the playing area and sub in and out as needed. At the whistle, throw the ball into the center of the playing area to begin the game. During the game, the athletes are permitted to move freely around the pool as long as they stay in the designated area (i.e., the shallow or deep end). Athletes score goals by throwing the ball into the opposing team's net. However, at least two athletes must touch the ball before scoring. If a goal is scored without the ball having touched other athletes, the score is voided and the opposing team takes possession of the ball. After each score, the athletes must rotate their positions (i.e., the goalie becomes a guard, a selected forward becomes the new goalie, and the guards become forwards). The game continues for two 15-minute halves. At halftime, allow the athletes to catch their breath for two to five minutes, get a drink, and rethink strategy. Teams also switch ends at halftime.

Note:

• A lifeguard is required for this activity.

Variations:

• The athletes can play using the length of the pool, rather than the width.

• Require the athletes to wear old shoes during play.

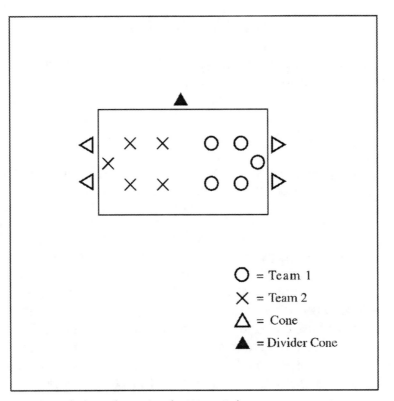

Set-up and player formation for Water Polo

#98: Water Weave

Skills Developed: Aerobic conditioning, agility, balance, coordination, muscular strength/endurance, and teamwork

Players: 6–12

Playing Area: Large open area (outside)

Materials Needed: 2 large trash cans/barrels free of holes, 2 large buckets, 10 cones, 2 sources of water (i.e., additional trash cans or 2 water hoses)

Description: Begin by placing two empty trash cans 20 to 40 yards from the starting line (the distance is determined by the type of athletes and their age). Between the starting line and the trash cans, position the cones in a straight line eight to 12 feet apart. Then, divide the athletes into two teams of equal strength and give each team a source of water and a bucket. At the whistle, the first athlete in line sprints to the water source (e.g., water hoses, trash cans of water), fills his bucket, and then quickly weaves in and out of the cones to the trash cans at the other end. The athlete then pours his bucket of water into the trash can and sprints back to his team to hand off the bucket. The process is repeated until the trash can is full, or until a predetermined height, or time limit, is reached. The first team to fill its trash can wins.

Variations:

- Use sand, dirt, rocks, or any loose heavy objects in place of the water. This game can also be used to the coach's advantage (e.g., to move dirt from one area to another to create a pitching mound).

- Instruct the athletes to walk a balance beam to get from one area to another. You can even create a zigzag pattern with the beams to add more difficulty to the challenge. Also, you can set up one set of cones or balance beams for the teams to share. This variation will cause a sense of urgency in the athletes to get to the obstacle first.

#99: Whammy Ball

Skills Developed: Aerobic conditioning, agility, coordination, reaction, and teamwork

Players: 8 or more

Playing Area: Volleyball or basketball court

Materials Needed: 1 volleyball (or volleyball trainer or beach ball) and volleyball nets

Description: Divide the athletes into four teams and divide the playing area into quarters by setting the nets up in the shape of a plus sign. The objective of the game is similar to volleyball. The athletes attempt to hit the ball over into the opponent's court. However, three different courts are available for the athletes to hit the ball into. Rather than scoring points, teams are given whammies for allowing the ball to land inside their court. Whammies are also given to a team that hits the ball out of play. The team with the lowest number of whammies wins. This game can be played for time or until a predetermined number of whammies has been attained.

Variations:

- Use volleyball scoring (i.e., rally).

- After a team receives a particular number of whammies, that team is out and must perform another task (e.g., calisthenics, sport-specific drills).

- Vary the techniques allowed to hit the ball over the net (e.g., feet, hands, head).

#100: Wheelbarrow Relay

Skills Developed: Muscular strength/endurance and stability

Players: 4 or more

Playing Area: Large open area (preferably a gymnasium)

Materials Needed: 2 markers or cones

Description: Divide the athletes into pairs. One athlete in each pair is designated as the wheel and the other athlete as the carrier. The wheel positions his hands on the floor and lifts his legs up behind him. The carrier then grabs the wheel's ankles and holds them close to his own hips. The wheel walks on his hands to a predetermined marker as the carrier follows behind holding his legs in the air. Upon reaching the marker on the opposite side of the playing area, the athletes switch positions and return to the starting point. The first team to reach the starting point wins.

Note:

- It is important that the standing athlete not push the wheel athlete. It is the wheel athlete who sets the pace.

Variations:

- Increase the distance traveled.

- Perform this game by traveling forward, backward, and laterally to increase the difficulty.

- The athletes can perform this relay through an obstacle course.

- Set up agility/speed ladders and require the athletes to position their hands in the boxes using various patterns traditionally used to develop footwork.

#101: X-Factor

Skills Developed: Anaerobic conditioning, agility, balance, coordination, muscular strength/endurance, power, reaction, and teamwork

Players: 12 or more

Playing Area: Large open area

Materials Needed: 2 large ropes approximately 20 feet in length and 5 cones/markers

Description: Begin by stretching out one rope and laying it in the middle of the playing area. Loop the remaining rope around the center of the first rope (making a large "X"). Next, position the cones three to five yards from each of the four ends of the rope along the perimeter of the playing area. After this preparation is done, divide the athletes into four teams of equal size and strength and instruct each team to pick up its end of the rope. At the whistle, each team of athletes begins to pull in an attempt to reach the cone sitting behind it. In the process, the athletes are challenged not only by frontal pulling but by lateral pulling as well. The first team that reaches their cone wins.

Variation:

- The variations used for a standard tug-of-war can easily be applied to this simple, yet challenging version (refer to #64 and #65 for examples).

References and Recommended Reading

Bompa, T.O. (2000). *Total Training for Young Champions*. Champaign, IL: Human Kinetics.

Chu, D.A., Faigenbaum, A.D., and Falkel, J.E. (2006). *Progressive Plyometrics for Kids*. Monterey, CA: Healthy Learning.

Dawes, J. (2005). *Exercises and Drills to Develop Agility*. Monterey, CA: Healthy Learning.

Dawes, J. (2005). *Exercises and Drills to Develop Static and Dynamic Balance*. Monterey, CA: Healthy Learning.

Dawes, J. (2005). *Exercises and Drills to Develop Neuromuscular Coordination*. Monterey, CA: Healthy Learning.

Foster, D.R., Overholt, J.L., and Shultz, R. (1989). *Indoor Action Games for Elementary Children: Active Games and Academic Activities for Fun and Fitness*. West Nyack, NY: Parker Publishing Company.

Gabbett, T.J. (2002). Training injuries in rugby league: An evaluation of skill-based conditioning games. *The Journal of Strength and Conditioning Research*, 16(2), 236–241.

Gambetta, V. (1998). *At the End of Endurance in the Gambetta Method*, 2nd ed. Sarasota, FL: Gambetta Sports Training Systems, Inc.

Gamble, P. (2004). A skill-based conditioning games approach to metabolic conditioning for elite rugby football players. *The Journal of Strength and Conditioning Research*, 18(3), 491–497.

Gustafson, M.A., Wolfe, S.K., and King, C. (1991). *Great Games for Young People*. Champaign, IL: Human Kinetics.

Jeffreys, I. (2005a). A multidimensional approach to enhancing recovery. *Strength and Conditioning Journal*, 27(5), 78–85.

Jeffreys, I. (2005b). Conditioning for field hockey: Small side games to improve. *Strength and Conditioning Journal*, 27(5), 78–85.

Jeffreys, I. (2004). The use of small-sided games in the metabolic training of high school soccer players. *Strength and Conditioning Journal*, 26(5), 77–78.

Metz, G. (2004). Agility antics. *Training & Conditioning Magazine*, 14(4), 23–33.

Morgan-Handzel, T. (2005). Training for the game: Conditioning games. *NSCA Performance Training Journal*, 4(6), 15–16.

Pangrazzi, R.P. (1998). *Dynamic Physical Education for Elementary School Children*. Boston, MA: Allyn & Bacon.

Plisk, S.S. & Gambetta, V. (1997). Tactical metabolic training: Part 1. *Strength and Conditioning*, 19(2), 44–53.

Sherman, M. (1998). The games wrestlers play. *Coach and Athletic Director*, 67(8), 96–98.

Wheeler, K. and Spilker, O.H. (1991). *Physical Education Curriculum Activities Kit for Grades K–6*. West Nyack, N.Y: Parker Publishing Company.

Wilmore, J.H. and Costill, D.L. (1999). *Physiology of Sport and Exercise*, 2nd ed. Champaign, IL: Human Kinetics.

About the Authors

Jay Dawes, M.S., is the director/owner of the 180 Center for Health and Performance in Edmond, Oklahoma, and is the strength coach for the USA Paralympic Sit-volleyball team. Dawes holds certifications through the National Strength and Conditioning Association as a certified personal trainer (NSCA-CPT*D), the American College of Sports Medicine as a health/fitness instructor (ACSM-HFI), the American Council on Exercise as a certified personal trainer, and the United States of America Weightlifting Federation as a club coach (USAW-CC). He is also a Ph.D. candidate at Oklahoma State University in the area of health and human performance/exercise science.

Dawes has been featured in a number of instructional videos, has authored numerous articles for industry publications, including the *Strength and Conditioning Journal*, *NSCA Performance Training Journal*, *Training and Conditioning Magazine*, and the *American College of Sports Medicine Certified Newsletter*, and is a frequent presenter at both the state and national levels. In addition, Dawes works with the National Strength and Conditioning Association in various capacities, including serving as the Oklahoma state director, a conference committee member, the personal trainers conference sub-committee chair, an executive council member for the Personal Trainers Special Interest Group (PTSIG), and as an editor for the *Strength and Conditioning Journal's* One-on-One Column. He resides in Edmond, Oklahoma, with his wife, April, and two daughters, Gabrielle and Addison.

Chris Mooney, M.S., is a member of the kinesiology and exercise studies department at Oklahoma City University and is the athletic enhancement/martial arts coordinator for the 180 Center for Health and Performance in Edmond, Oklahoma. He received his master's degree from the University of Central Oklahoma in wellness management with an emphasis in exercise science. Mooney is certified by the National Strength and Conditioning Association as a strength and conditioning specialist (CSCS*D) and personal trainer (NSCA-CPT*D), and by the United States of America Weightlifting Federation as a club coach (USAW-CC). In addition, Mooney is a regular speaker for the Oklahoma Strength and Conditioning Association (OSCA) on various topics related to personal training, athletic performance enhancement, and martial arts. He resides in Oklahoma City with his wife, Jennifer.